Museum Ex

In recent years, museums have developed into multi-dimensional organizations, displaying, preserving and collecting objects which are of increasing interest to the global community. They have adapted to a consumer-oriented world and now compete for our attention with other "leisure-time" activities. They must prove themselves worthy of the visitor's time and attention by developing quality exhibitions.

Museum Exhibition: Theory and Practice is the only textbook of its kind to consider exhibition development from an integrated approach from theory to practice. The field of exhibition preparation is a complex and demanding one, calling on a variety of professional skills. Designers must have creative ability and aesthetic sense as well as considerable skills in writing, management and interpretation. David Dean examines a wide range of exhibition development concerns, including planning and design of exhibitions, collection care of exhibits, display evaluation and administration, content and text development for exhibitions and computer usage.

Museum Exhibition provides a complete outline for all those concerned with providing displays for museums and similar cultural heritage concerns. It will be essential reading for all museum professionals.

David Dean is the Assistant Director for Operations and Adjunct Professor in the Museum Science Program at the Museum of Texas Tech University in Lubbock, Texas. He teaches communications and interpretation in the program and oversees the museum's exhibitions division. Mr Dean has been involved in exhibition design and production for eighteen years in the respective roles of preparator, designer, production manager and administrator. He is the co-author, with Gary Edson, of *The Handbook for Museums* (1994).

The Heritage: Care–Preservation–Management programme has been designed to serve the needs of the museum and heritage community worldwide. It publishes books and information services for professional museum and heritage workers, and for all the organizations that service the museum community.

Museum Exhibition

Theory and Practice

David Dean

London and New York

First published 1994
by Routledge
11 New Fetter Lane, London EC4P 4EE

Simultaneously published in the USA and Canada
by Routledge
29 West 35th Street, New York, NY 10001

First published in paperback 1996

Reprinted in 1998, 2000

Routledge is an imprint of the Taylor & Francis Group

Typeset in Sabon by
Florencetype Ltd, Stoodleigh, Devon

Printed and bound in Great Britain by
Butler & Tanner Ltd, Frome, Somerset

Printed on acid free paper

British Library Cataloguing in Publication Data
A catalogue record for this book is available from the British Library

Library of Congress Cataloguing in Publication Data
Dean, David
Museum exhibition : theory and practice / David Dean.
p.   cm.
Includes bibliographical references and index.
1. Exhibitions. 2. Museum techniques. I. Title.
AM151.D43 1993
069'.5–dc20 93-24653

ISBN 0–415–08016–9 (hbk)
ISBN 0–415–08017–7 (pbk)

To the students of the art of exhibition, everywhere.

Contents

Illustrations

Acknowledgments

Products are often the result of activity driven by need. This book is a product that resulted from the need to have a text for teaching exhibition design. The students of the Museum Science Program (Museum of Texas Tech University) provided the initial need that triggered the activity. My thanks to them and to the institution.

Activity requires support to prosper. The museum director, Gary Edson, provided much of the support, both intellectually and operationally, that made the product possible. My thanks to him.

Activity also requires time to realize the product. I offer my special thanks to my understanding wife, Sue, and my children, Kendra and Daniel, for their support in this effort, and for freely giving of the time that rightfully was theirs.

Introduction

Museums began as human society's equivalent of cultural memory banks. Through the years they have evolved into much more. Though the prime medium is tangible objects, the essential value of collections is the information contained in them and what it means to the global community. Other institutions deal in information also, but only museums uniquely collect, preserve, research, and publicly display objects as an essential function of their existence.

In the later part of the twentieth century, museums have become multi-faceted, multi-purposed, and multi-dimensional organizations. The era of the user-friendly resource is in full stride; the Information Age is upon us. Museums have had to adapt to this consumer-oriented world to compete with other, so-called "leisure-time" activities. Whether one agrees that leisure is a correct classification for former "temples of learning" is a matter of opinion. Regardless of one's viewpoint, museums do exist as optional elements in the majority of the population's daily lifestyles. As an option, museums must prove themselves worthy of the visitor's attention and time.

In the past few decades, museums have seen significant improvements in collection care and use, and in the fields of exhibition presentation and public programming. The level of knowledge about nearly every technical aspect of the museum field is expanding constantly. New fields and sub-disciplines are opening up and evolving. The museum of the next century may be very different from the ones we now know. However, one aspect has always been, remains, and will probably continue to be fundamental to the museum institutional identity: public exhibitions.

The field of exhibition development and preparation is a complex and demanding one. Many subjects and disciplines are involved that must be mastered and their terminologies understood. Designers need a positive attitude toward and a creative ability for problem solving. They must have the desire to communicate ideas to others, a well-developed aesthetic sense, and considerable skills in writing, management, computer use, and interpretation. Increasingly, knowledge about audiences, traffic control, and educational goals is needed.

Obviously not every person entering the museum profession is either trained or talented in all aspects of the exhibition process, nor are they always inclined toward making exhibitions a career. However, exhibitions are rarely the product of one individual. They require teamwork involving all museum specialities. In museums where one or two persons constitute the entire exhibition design and production resources, knowledge is a powerful tool for achieving success. General knowledge of exhibition theories, methodologies, and practices is the best tool that an exhibition team member in any size of organization can acquire. This book aims to provide the interested reader with an overview of those areas where knowledge is needed to accomplish the institutional goals.

The museum exhibition mission

While profit may not be the specific motive, museums have the desire to "sell" the institution, change attitudes, modify behavior, and increase conformity (of knowledge). All are viable and reasonable goals for museums.

The main difference between commercial or public-service exhibits and museum exhibitions lies in the motive or mission of the respective organizations. The term commercial exhibit is self-defining. It has as a goal the selling of a product or services for financial gain. A public-service exhibit is likewise obvious in its meaning: informing the public and changing attitudes and behaviors. However, is the term museum exhibition as obvious? It is, if the word "museum" is considered. Museum means a dwelling for the Muses – a place for study, reflection, and learning. Therefore, museum exhibitions are self-defining as well. They have the mission to provide places for education and reflection.

The museological motivation for exhibiting is to provide the objects and information necessary for learning to occur. Exhibitions fulfill, in part, the museum institutional mission by exposing collections to view, thus affirming the public's trust in the institution as caretaker of the societal record. Museum exhibitions also accomplish several other goals. These include:

- Promoting community interest in the museum by offering alternative leisure activities where individuals or groups may find worthwhile experiences.
- Supporting the institution financially: exhibitions help the museum as a whole justify its existence and its expectation for continued support. Donors, both public and private, are more likely to give to a museum with an active and popular exhibition schedule.
- Providing proof of responsible handling of collections if a donor wishes to give objects. Properly presented exhibitions confirm public trust in the museum as a place for conservation and careful preservation. Potential donors of objects or collections will be much more inclined to place their treasures in institutions that will care for the objects properly, and will present those objects for public good in a thoughtful and informative manner.

In general, a healthy and well-presented public exhibitions program affords an institution credibility to its supporting community and to the broader community of museums. Exhibitions have the intent to advance the institutional mission by exposing collections to public view, providing enlightening and educational experiences, and proving the public trust. Further, the specific goals of museum exhibitions involve the desire to change attitudes, modify behavior, and increase the availability of knowledge.

> **"For the visitor, the exhibit environment *is* the primary medium of communication."[1]**

Types of exhibits

For clarification, it is wise to define terms. The words "exhibit," "exhibition," and "display" all have rather arbitrary meanings that vary from institution to institution, person to person. As dictionary definitions are of little help in solving these semantic differences, it is necessary to continue the arbitrary tradition of defining terms. For the purposes of this book, the word "display" will generally refer to a presentation of objects for public view without significant interpretation added. "Exhibit" will usually mean the localized grouping of objects and interpretive materials that form a cohesive unit within a gallery. "Exhibition" will be used to allude to a comprehensive grouping of all elements (including exhibits and displays) that form a complete public presentation of collections and information for the public use.

It is generally assumed that museum exhibitions incorporate collection objects, or their representations, as the primary channels of communication. However, that is not always true. Some museum-related displays may incorporate few or no objects at all. These presentations are informational in content and intent. There are legitimate uses and reasons for this form of display, but by and large, the uniqueness of museum exhibitions rests in their employment of the "real thing."

Intent or purpose lies with the exhibit maker. Exhibitions range from being either object-oriented at one extreme, to concept-oriented at the other. That is, either objects or messages predominate. The scale in Figure 0.1, adapted from diagram 9 in Verhaar and Meeter's *Project Model Exhibitions*,[2] illustrates this idea:

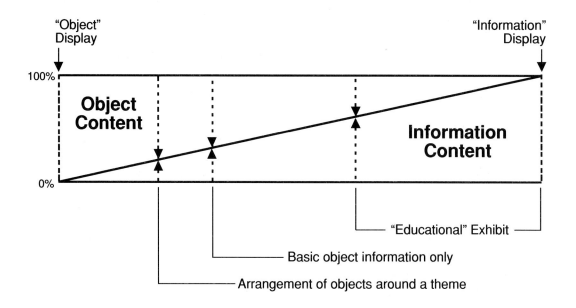

0.1 Exhibit content scale

- At one end is the object display. This is a presentation of objects purely for the objects' sake; no interpretive information is involved. It is like setting a collection of vases or ceramic figures on a shelf in a home. The intent is simply to arrange the objects attractively, relying upon them to speak for themselves.
- At the other extreme is the information display in which objects are either not present or of minimal importance. This kind of presentation depends upon text and graphics to get its message across, much as a book does. The intent is to communicate an idea or ideas that the exhibitor has determined are in the viewers' best interest to know.

Along the diagram's diagonal line is where one finds most exhibitions. The relative dominance of one aspect or the other determines whether an exhibition is more object- or concept-oriented. Possible and common combinations are:

- The object-oriented exhibition in which collections are central. Educational information is limited. Relationships, values, and hidden or implied meanings are not examined to any significant degree. The exhibition maker focuses on a direct aesthetic or a classification approach to presentation – art is often presented in this way.
- The concept-oriented exhibition is one where attention is focused on the message and the transfer of information rather than on the collections. The aim is to transmit a message regardless of whether collections are available to assist interpretation or for illustration. Text, graphics, photographs, and

other didactic materials play a dominant role. The main advantages of this type of presentation over a book are the elements of size and wider exposure.

In the middle ground there are exhibitions that recognize the dual museum missions to collect objects and to use them to educate.

- Thematic exhibitions, closer to the object-oriented end of the scale, use collections arranged around a theme with basic information provided, such as a title sign and identification and caption labels. For instance, in an exhibition featuring works of Pablo Picasso, the pieces might be exhibited with only basic information, relying upon the artist's reputation and available distributional materials and catalogs to impart what interpretive details are considered desirable.
- Closer to the concept-oriented end are "educational" exhibitions that incorporate about 60 percent information and 40 percent objects (see Figure 0.1). Textual information is heavily relied upon to assist in transmitting the exhibition message.

It is important to note that no sharp line of demarcation exists between the two ends of the scale, and that none of the combinations is inherently right or wrong. Planning decisions about the type of exhibition to have must be based upon what message is to be communicated and what combination of objects and information will do the job most effectively. Such choices ought to be deliberate and founded upon the goals of the institution and the developers' knowledge of their target audiences.

Arguably, since a museum's primary milieu is the "real thing," it might be assumed that all that is required is to place objects on public view and let them speak for themselves. When interpretation and communication are minimal, leaving presentation dominant, the result is what is called "open storage." This form of exhibitry hearkens back to an earlier, largely obsolete display methodology. In particular instances and for specific purposes, there is still validity for open storage as a display strategy.

However, what does a painting, a bone, or a rock communicate in and of itself? Is the story behind the object always the main point, or is the emotional impact the main objective? These are questions to consider when making decisions about the kind of exhibition to pursue.

The role of interpretation

As museums have moved into a more proactive stance toward their parent communities in this century, the educational mission has become a primary focus of exhibitions. This has meant that the stoically static exhibitry of the past has given way to active efforts to communicate the information contained in collections. How much of its underlying history or meaning does a painting reveal without interpretation? The information behind an object must be related to the viewer through a planned and directed explanation for it to have meaning.

> **Interpretation is the act or process of explaining or clarifying, translating, or presenting a personal understanding about a subject or object.**

The desires that museum exhibitors have for communication vary from museum to museum, exhibit to exhibit, and community to community. However, some messages can be reasonably well identified as being common to most museum exhibition efforts.

One such message is that museums are places to encounter actual objects – the "real thing." Exhibitions allow the public at least a near approach to the collections. This has the effect of stimulating curiosity and interest. The value of being in the presence of Leonardo da Vinci's *Mona Lisa* or the skeletal remains of a *Tyrannosaurus rex* is unquestionable, though incalculable. The hoped-for results might be fostering a sensitivity to art or science, and learning as a whole realm of human experience. How do such aspirations relate to exhibitions of farm equipment or Stone Age tools? The desired results are the same: engendering interests and curiosity that will develop into long-term personal growth and enrichment.

In addition to the rather intangible benefits afforded by exhibitions at a personal level, there are the broader ones available to public institutions and to the museum itself. As an alternative educational partner for schools, museums are invaluable and unparalleled. Coordination between exhibition goals and school curricula can be extremely beneficial. Bringing subject matter to life, in a tangible way, is what museum exhibitions excel at doing. A museum visit can do much to stimulate a student's lifelong interest in a subject.

Museum exhibitions offer an enjoyable means of assimilating information, sometimes of great complexity. The fact of viewing the real thing is, in itself, intellectually pleasing for many people. The opportunity to view objects in relaxed, comfortable surroundings where interaction between the viewer and the object, the student and the teacher, visitor and docent, and the pupils and their peers can occur, leads to retention and internalizing of an otherwise academic topic. It is far more rewarding to view an actual pre-Columbian figure, than simply to read about it in a book and look at a picture. The effect of doing both fosters lasting impressions and increased retention of knowledge gained.

The entertainment value of exhibitions should not be overlooked, either. Again, communication occurring in a relaxed, enjoyable environment promotes willingness to learn and to continue learning. The "Gee whiz!" factor is part of this entertainment aspect. Things that are big, famous, real, or impressive in some sense are readily and eagerly examined by most people. When a person's attention is captured, study occurs. When study is guided by interesting and understandable labeling or docenting, learning occurs without duress or discomfort.

Conclusions

The museological mission of education is accomplished in large part by presenting public exhibitions. Information presented in ways that excite curiosity and stimulate the desire to learn results in people responding positively to the activity of learning. When the patron exits an exhibition with the sense that he or she is personally enriched for having made the effort to visit, then for that individual, the museum goal is attained. For, not only will he or she have a positive attitude about learning, they will have gained knowledge and understanding as well.

Museums are institutions for social as well as academic enlightenment. They provide non-confrontational and eclectic venues for expressing ideas that are sometimes, themselves, controversial. As forums for free expression, exhibitions are ideal. They are based upon the tangible evidence of the cultural and scientific progression of humankind. Presented in an environment that allows the viewers to learn, reflect, and assimilate the world at their own pace, the baggage of preconceptions and biases can be dispelled and new, enlightened attitudes engendered.

Unlike formalized public education, museums are always available. There is no age or intellectual prerequisite. Everyone is welcome, indeed encouraged, to share in the wealth of human accomplishment represented by museum collections. Whether a small grouping of local heritage memorabilia, or a vast assemblage of artistic and scientific artifacts, all museums need the outlet of exhibitions to make their treasures available to the people who support and derive benefit from them.

1

The exhibition development process

Approaches to planning

Institutions and organizations such as museums are much like the proverbial iceberg. Most of the substance lies below the surface, hidden from view. Nearly all museums depend upon public use and approval to justify their places within society, so there is a real need for demonstration of the richness of those hidden depths. Exhibitions and programs are the principle public expressions of the heart of museums: the collections.

The popular understanding of exhibitions does not recognize or appreciate the inner mechanisms required to prepare and present them. Like Athena leaping full-grown from the head of Zeus, there is a mythical quality to the ease with which exhibitions appear in public. However, as with any project, exhibitions require much planning and management to realize the end product. Over time, the sequence of events and efforts that produce public exhibitions has become established. The procedural elements in planning and executing any project are universal, regardless of the end product. The main difference between creating an exhibition and preparing a sales strategy or building an automobile is the mission of the organization undertaking the project.

In commercial affairs, accomplishing tasks is a highly organized operation. The systematized approach used by businesses to manage their projects can be quite valuable if related to exhibition development. That is because any course of action with a product as its final goal is a project. As the process used in producing commercial products has proven to be effective, museums have adopted the methodology, and even the terminology, of business to describe the equivalent developmental steps in making exhibitions. Understanding the process is easier when outlined as a series of phases and subordinate stages.

All projects, regardless of their beginning or intended outcome, share common traits. The time it takes to plan, develop, and execute the project is limited. Projects are cyclical. They have beginnings that arise from ideas generated from former activities, and after running their courses, they generate new approaches and ideas for future projects.

As Figure 1.1 shows, a project may be illustrated as a series of events along a line of time. This is called a project model.[1] It is easy to see how an exhibition's development fits into such a model.

1.1 Exhibition project model

The progressive, sequential nature of the project model works well with museum exhibition development. The sequential arrangement of phases and stages may be outlined to make types of activities and specific tasks more easily discernible. Throughout development, and in each phase, there are three principle tasking areas. They are:

- Product-oriented activities – efforts centered on the collection objects and their interpretation.
- Management-oriented activities – tasks that focus on providing resources and personnel necessary to completing the project.
- Coordination activities – keeping the product- and management-oriented activities working toward the same goal.

OUTLINE OF EXHIBITION DEVELOPMENT

Conceptual phase

- Product-oriented activities:

collecting ideas
comparing ideas with audience needs and the museum's mission
selecting projects to develop
- Management activities:
    assessing available resources to do the project
- Results:
    a schedule of exhibitions
    identification of potential or available resources

Developmental phase

Planning stage

- Product-oriented activities:
    setting goals for the exhibition
    writing the storyline
    designing the physical exhibition
    creating an educational plan
    researching promotional strategies
- Management activities:
    estimating costs
    investigating sources and applying for funding
    establishing resource budgets
    appointing tasks
- Results:
    an exhibition plan
    an educational plan
    a promotional plan

Production stage

- Product-oriented activities:
    preparing the exhibition components
    mounting and installing the collection objects
    developing the educational programs and training docents
    implementing the promotional plan
- Management activities:
    overseeing the availability and use of resources
    tracking progress and coordinating activities
- Results:
    presenting the exhibition to the public
    using the educational programs with the exhibition

Functional phase

Operational stage

- Product-oriented activities:
    presenting the exhibition to the public on a regular basis
    implementing the educational programs
    conducting visitor surveys

    maintaining the exhibition
    providing security for the exhibition
- Management activities:
    settling accounts
    administration of personnel and services
- Results:
    achieving the exhibition goals
    preventing deterioration of collections

Terminating stage

- Product-oriented activities:
    dismantling the exhibition
    returning objects to the collection storage
    documenting collection handling
- Management activities:
    balancing accounts
- Results:
    the exhibition is ended
    the collections are returned
    the gallery is cleared and repaired

Assessment phase

- Product-oriented activities:
    assessing the exhibition
    assessing the development process
- Management activities:
    creating an evaluation report
- Results:
    an evaluation report
    suggested improvements to the product and the process

The application of the models and the outline to the actual process of exhibition development will be clearer if each part is examined separately. It is important to note that, although dissecting the process provides useful handles to grasp ideas by, the real activities are not always so clearly delineated. Often activities flow together and mix with each other as the project progresses.

Conceptual phase

To embark upon a detailed exploration of exhibition development, we must begin with its inception. Exhibitions start as ideas that come from many sources. Listed are some frequently encountered:

- audience suggestions
- board members or trustees
- collections management personnel
- community leaders

11

- curators
- current events
- director
- educators
- staff and volunteers

Ideas for exhibitions are not always conceived in an orderly fashion and often arrive with a variety of personal agendas attached. A patron, staff or board member may see an exhibition at another museum, watch a program on television, or read a magazine, and thus become motivated to propose an exhibition topic. The experiences of individuals, the assessed needs of a community, or a new collection acquisition may provide the impetus for exhibiting. In some cases, the need to replace other exhibitions will prompt the search for new ideas and themes.

In all cases, the motivations to exhibit should emanate from a prevailing predisposition toward serving the public. Museums should be like leaky vessels or sponges in their communities. Ideas should seep in from all directions and be sifted constantly, searching for those that fulfill the criteria of public service and education. It is not appropriate for exhibitions to arise solely as outlets for self-aggrandizement by staff or board members. Often an initiator's exuberance for his or her idea leaps ahead of thoughtful consideration or careful planning. Failure to channel enthusiasm into a cooperative organizational process may lead to a chaotic and frustrating mixture of conflicting communication and confused goals. The outcome will be lack of focus, disaffection, dissatisfaction, and inferior exhibitions.

To avoid such a regrettable condition the administration needs to place the role and function of the museum foremost. Responsible collection care, and properly assessing the needs of the museum's public are at the heart of conscientious exhibitions and interpretive programs. However and wherever ideas may arise, a phased development plan permits everyone involved to see their part in the process with clarity.

Though ideas arise in many ways from multiple sources, there must be decisions made as to which to pursue or discard. Organizations develop approaches to decision-making that work for them. These approaches have many variations rendering a single set of criteria too restrictive to be useful to all organizations. However, it is vital that decisions be made based upon a well-defined sub-set of public-oriented criteria, rather than on personal biases.

Ideally, short- and long-range plans that incorporate the museum mission, constituency needs, educational goals, scope of collections, and available resources are a part of the organizational documentation arsenal. Established standards ensure that choices are responsible. At the administrative level, a regularly reviewed written exhibition policy should be a priority. Appointing a committee to do initial research and provide advice can be helpful as well. Formulating exhibition strategies using foundational instruments will meet constituency needs. Lack of definition in planning exhibition programs will lead to a museum being driven by the demand to fill space, rather than by ethical purpose and educational design.

The current consensus of the role of museums in their communities rests upon twin cornerstones: accountability to a constituency, and adherence to accepted professional museum standards. Arbitrary, unilateral choices in exhibition topics are not acceptable to a public with other leisure options. Personal preferences of staff or board members are not adequate foundations upon which to build an exhibition program. Even in small museums, where staffs are small and often voluntary, the decision-making process needs to be clearly set down and the development of an exhibition program founded upon a recognition of community needs and professionalism.

An understanding of community needs and expectations comes from audience assessment. A serious and common mistake is basing decisions about exhibition programs on internal assumptions about community needs, rather than on information gathered from the community itself. Obtaining such knowledge requires time, skills, and energies both to collect and to keep it current. These resources are often unavailable to largely volunteer governing boards. Professional consultants or staff members versed in the methodologies and techniques of community assessment are the proper parties to develop and apply exhibition assessment criteria. In many communities, chambers of commerce have already done visitor surveys, and demographic and psycho-graphic studies. They are usually quite willing to make such information available to public-oriented institutions.

Having gained a working knowledge of community needs and expectations, and armed with the museum mission statement and exhibition policy, the task is to evaluate the suggested exhibitions. Using the knowledge and documents as filters and guides, a slate of exhibitions can be generated that demonstrates sensitivity toward constituency needs and expectations, while adhering to institutional goals and standards.

Conceptual phase activities can be viewed as product- and management-oriented, although not as clearly as the later phases. Conceptual phase product-oriented activities can be summarized as:

● Gathering ideas.
● Assessing the ideas within the framework of the museum's mission, its policies, and community needs.
● Selecting an exhibition for development.

Management-oriented activities include:

● Approving and scheduling the exhibition for development.
● Assessing available or potential resources.

The results of conceptual phase activities should be the scheduling of the exhibition and the identification of the resources needed to present it.

Development phase

Exhibition development is a process aimed at realizing an idea – giving it flesh and bones. Much of the energy of a staff will be directed toward product-related goals. However, management activities are essential as well. Management duties center upon procurement, distribution, and regulation of resources. This involves the following:

- time management
- money management
- quality control
- communication
- organizational control – assigning tasks

Neither product- nor management-oriented activities can function properly without the other. It is the combined efforts of those people active in both areas of endeavor that produce the result: the exhibition.

After the decision to develop an exhibition is made, ideas need to be translated into actions moving toward realizable goals. The director decides who to include in the planning process based on the requisite disciplines and skills. Whether the project is accomplished by a team of several people, or by only one or two individuals, the essential tasks remain the same. Only the scope and breadth of the job changes based upon the time available to accomplish it. In some instances, only one or two people are available, and tailoring the size of the project to fit resources is necessary.

Normally, those roles required in product-oriented tasks include the curator, educator, and designer. The curator or expert in the exhibition's subject does research, provides scholarly information, and selects and curates the appropriate collection objects. To guide interpretive planning and presentation, a team member with an educational background and training is needed. The educator advises about educational needs related to the design, develops information for tours and programs, and provides training for docents and guides. Another member is needed to translate the subject, objects, and ideas into visual form: the designer. The designer takes the information provided by other team members and creates a plan for presenting it to the public.

From the management side, a person is needed to oversee and coordinate planning and resources: a project manager. His or her purpose is to act as a person who facilitates – who encourages communication, sees that information and resources are available as needed, calls meetings and assigns tasks as required, and acts as a mediator when necessary. Most often, this task is not painful or stressful. However, the project manager needs to be an experienced professional to handle difficulties if they arise. Attached to the project manager's job may be periodic progress reports to the director or governing authority.

Technical advisors may be required for complex or specialized activities. Conservators may be consulted for collection management purposes.

Marketing specialists may be employed depending upon the scope of the exhibition and the target audience. In effect, the exhibition planning team should be configured to fit the need. The larger the team, the more complex communication and consensus become. On the other hand, appropriate levels of expertise should be included to do the job properly.

Planning stage

The planning stage sets the standards for building the final exhibition. Without spending appropriate time and effort at this point, the rest of the development process stands a good chance of being confusing at best, and at worst, resulting in a poorly executed exhibition lacking in content and direction.

Exhibition developers draw upon constituency surveys to determine the exhibition's target group or groups. Developing and setting down exhibition goals based upon a target audience will help clarify objectives. From these goals flow an identifiable set of criteria against which later to rate exhibition effectiveness.

After exhibition goals and objectives are established, the more concrete, object-oriented work of research, script-writing, designing, and formulating educational and promotional plans may proceed.

During the planning stage, management activities are critical and centered around budgeting. Budgeting refers to the "Big Three": time, personnel and money. These are essential to realizing exhibition goals. For example, giving someone a task carries with it the responsibility to provide available time by setting deadlines. When staff members are working in one place, they cannot be elsewhere. In most museums, there are more jobs to accomplish than people to do them. This makes time-budgeting an imperative for efficiently employing skills and energies. However, without funding and procurement, work cannot go forward. Cost estimates must be compiled, funding sources located and secured, budgets set, and an accounting system created to keep track of funds in a consistent and timely manner.

The result of all these activities is a plan of action for producing the exhibition. The exhibition plan should include a timeline, a working budget, the storyline, a conservation and maintenance schedule, design drawings and schematics, the education goals and plans, and promotional or marketing strategies.

Production stage

The production stage is the time in an exhibition's cycle that involves the greatest amount of activity, and requires the most coordination of efforts. At this stage there are several product-oriented activities to be completed. They include:

- An assessment by the curator or collection manager setting forth the level of preliminary conservation required.
- A statement of requirements for the type and degree of support required and what environmental parameters are acceptable (light levels, relative humidity, temperature, etc.).
- A schedule for rotating collection objects off exhibition, and a maintenance plan.
- Negotiating and making arrangements for loans and contracts.
- Documenting the condition of the collection and its movement during the objects' transfer from storage to exhibition.
- Making transportation arrangements for some objects or people as required.
- Writing, checking, and preparing label, text, and title wording for production.
- Fabrication activities – preparing mounting structures for collection objects, preparing gallery space and environmental controls to meet specifications, producing printed materials and graphic images, and the construction of exhibit cases and vitrines.
- Development of educational and public programs, including the preparation of printed instructional materials for the gallery or as pre- or post-visit educational supplements. Other tasks might include preparing materials and training docents, and coordinating with speakers and demonstrators.
- Promotional activities such as writing press releases, issuing press packets, coordinating with media for press conferences or special photographic sessions. Other activities might be designing and implementing publicity strategies such as renting billboards, distributing posters or pamphlets, or arranging for paid advertisements.
- Installing the exhibition – the act of actualizing or executing the exhibition design. This includes erecting display structures such as walls and panels, installing environmental monitoring devices, and placing support elements and collection objects in the gallery space. Positioning wayfinders, labeling objects, installing barriers, and providing instructions to security and main-tenance personnel for the proper care of the exhibition are necessary as well.

Management activities during the production stage center on controlling the availability of resources and keeping track of their use. This involves:

- Budgetary control and account maintenance during fabrication – making purchases of construction materials and paying for services such as construction and conservation activities.
- Progress control, requiring periodic checks, meetings, and reports as necessary to determine the status of the project.
- Quality checks are needed to ensure that predetermined standards are met.
- Administrative activities, including expenditure approvals, approval and monitoring of changes, and providing appropriate personnel management.

The results of production stage activities should be:

- An exhibition open to the public of the quality and scope initially set forth as desirable.
- Instructions for proper care and maintenance of the exhibition, which should be available and disseminated to the proper departments and persons.
- Functional programs such as school tours, guided tours, and public events, which should be ready to be implemented.

Functional phase

After the exhibition is open to the public, it enters the functional phase. Under this heading are two stages. The first is the operational stage, which includes the daily activities of running and managing the exhibition.

Operational stage

Product-oriented activities include:

- Operating the exhibition, which might involve ticketing and admissions procedures. Also of major importance are the maintenance of the gallery and collections, seeing to the security and safety of staff and visitors, and monitoring conservation factors.
- Implementing the programs, tours, lectures, demonstrations, and any extra-museum activities such as trunk exhibits and outreach programs.
- Evaluation activities such as visitor surveys, pre- and post-visit questionnaires, informal observations, and related tasks. These need to be generated while the exhibition is functioning to provide data so that the exhibition's success or failure can be assessed at a later date.

Operational stage management activities include:

- Settling accounts.
- Administration of personnel and services.

The result of the operational stage should be the accomplishment of the educational objectives set forth during planning. The prime outcome from a collection management standpoint is to ensure that no significant deterioration occurs in the collection objects while they are on exhibit.

Terminating stage

Following the operational stage and concluding the exhibition's public life are activities that may be called the terminating stage. Product-oriented activities include:

- Dismantling the exhibition.
- Documenting the transfer of collection objects back to storage.
- Packing collection objects for return to lending institutions or for sending on to the next venue.

Terminating stage management activities involve:

- Balancing accounts to assess the proper use of funds and for reporting to granting agencies.

The results are that the exhibition is ended, collections are returned to their proper places, and galleries are cleared and made ready for the next exhibition.

Assessment phase

The final and an extremely important phase in exhibition development has to do with assessment. Evaluation is increasingly useful to museums for determining whether or not goals set early in the process were indeed accomplished. The process of assessment also serves to point the way to future exhibitions, improvements in methods and technologies, strategies, and goal-setting. Evaluation, too, is both product- and management-oriented.

Product-oriented activities are:

- Assessment of the exhibition from a product point-of-view. Determining how well the exhibition accomplished the educational and public goals set for it, how extensively it was visited and utilized, and whether or not the maintenance activities were adequate to protect the collections.
- Determining the success of the process in planning and executing the exhibition, or process assessment.

Assessment management activities include:

- The production of an evaluation report that sets down the findings of the product and process assessments.
- The preparation of an evaluation report – some granting agencies require such a report to assess the proper use and effectiveness of their funding.

The outcome of the assessment phase is to document the evaluation with a written report. However, the real value of assessment is improving the product and process for the next exhibition, and the engendering of new ideas for the future.

2

Audiences and learning

People and museums

People are the only reason for museums to exist. It may appear simplistic and obvious to say so, but that fact is sometimes overlooked in the day-to-day process of operating a museum. Everything museological revolves around the human race. Therefore, an understanding of human learning – or at least the basis for educated guessing – is useful for developing exhibitions that serve audience needs.

Knowing who the people are that museums serve has become a quest of the later part of the twentieth century. "Know your audience and market accordingly." This statement might well be the watchword of museums today, though some might not view it in quite such materialistic and commercial terms. However, even the most altruistic of museum professionals must acknowledge that knowing for whom the museum is being operated helps in planning exhibitions.

Of all the factors affecting decision-making in museums, the audience is the least understood and most frustrating. This is because people are themselves complex and unpredictable. We humans have managed to amass some information about how we function physically, physiologically, and emotionally. This knowledge can be valuable to the museum planner who wants to attract and hold an audience by providing meaningful experiences.

Much of the knowledge now available to museum professionals flows naturally from the art and science of education, which, in turn, derives many of its understandings from the fields of medicine and psychology. It is reasonable to apply such knowledge to museums because they are, at the core, educational institutions. Understanding how people learn and their requirements for having profitable educational experiences has proven to be of great help to museum exhibitors. Often such information assists in explaining observed, but puzzling human behaviors in museums (i.e., the need to touch, the tendency to avoid some galleries and to be irresistibly drawn to others, and the apparently positive response to some stimuli and the relative indifference toward others). Always, an understanding of audience needs and expectations will enhance both the process and the product of exhibitions.

Targeting audiences

Anticipating visitor needs and tendencies demands a clear notion of which groups to apply resources toward attracting. Museums should always be open to identifying and attracting new audiences, those beyond their existing visitorship. Awareness of community attitudes and expectations should be an ongoing process. As this base of information grows, and other factors such as demographics, educational levels, and economic stresses within a society change, a museum staff needs to evaluate its visitorship periodically. Self-examination to decide upon future audience development is a healthy process for museums. Community awareness and self-evaluation lead to identifying groups of individuals who are linked by common threads such as culture, leisure preferences, fields of study, ethnic or social affiliations, disabilities, socio-economic levels, and so forth. Any identifiable sub-group within a community is potentially a museum target audience. It is through careful study that responsible decisions about committing precious museum resources to reaching any new group are made.

Building a reliable, comprehensive profile of the community will assist in determining target audiences, their needs, and their expectations. Valuable methods of gathering this information include:

- Close examination of existing demographic and psychographic analyses, usually obtainable at chambers of commerce, and from commercial and governmental agencies.
- Interviewing individuals, civic groups and leaders.
- Forming and listening to focus groups from various community segments.

A decision to proceed with targeting any special group needs to be based upon two principal concerns:

- The belief that a benefit is attainable by the audience from the museum.
- The probable effectiveness of efforts to attract and hold a target audience.

Categorizing people, even into general groups, is an undertaking charged with problems and pitfalls, such as stereotyping, labeling, and unfair biasing. Museums are, or should be, one of the most democratic of institutions within any society, showing no preference or prejudice toward anyone, and serving the good of all. However, it is imperative to make practical judgments about the allocation of limited resources. Therefore, using objective criteria and recognizing the possibility of bias can allow some careful, helpful classification of people.

Two rational models may help provide a general summary of communities while avoiding unnecessarily subjective assessments. These are Arnold's Values and Lifestyles Segments (VALS) model (Figure 2.1),[1] and Maslow's Hierarchy of Human Needs (Figure 2.2).[2]

VALS (Values and Lifestyles Segments)

The VALS Double Hierarchy of Psychological Maturity

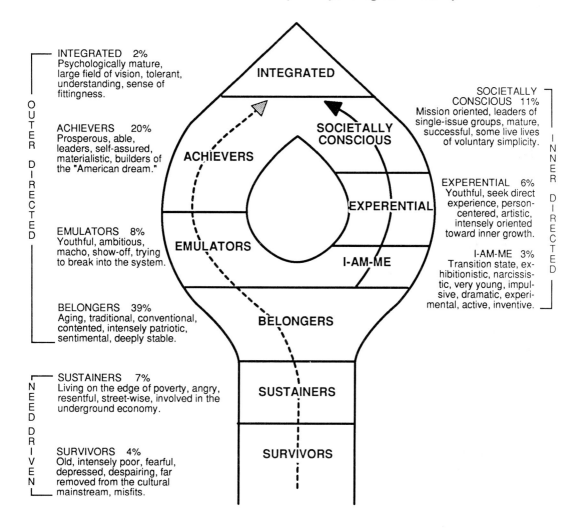

INTEGRATED 2%
Psychologically mature,
large field of vision, tolerant,
understanding, sense of
fittingness.

ACHIEVERS 20%
Prosperous, able,
leaders, self-assured,
materialistic, builders of
the "American dream."

EMULATORS 8%
Youthful, ambitious,
macho, show-off, trying
to break into the system.

BELONGERS 39%
Aging, traditional, conventional,
contented, intensely patriotic,
sentimental, deeply stable.

SUSTAINERS 7%
Living on the edge of poverty, angry,
resentful, street-wise, involved in the
underground economy.

SURVIVORS 4%
Old, intensely poor, fearful,
depressed, despairing, far
removed from the cultural
mainstream, misfits.

OUTER DIRECTED

NEED DRIVEN

SOCIETALLY
CONSCIOUS 11%
Mission oriented, leaders of
single-issue groups, mature,
successful, some live lives
of voluntary simplicity.

EXPERIENTIAL 6%
Youthful, seek direct
experience, person-
centered, artistic,
intensely oriented
toward inner growth.

I-AM-ME 3%
Transition state, ex-
hibitionistic, narcissis-
tic, very young, impul-
sive, dramatic, experi-
mental, active, inventive.

INNER DIRECTED

2.1 Values and Lifestyles Segments model

21

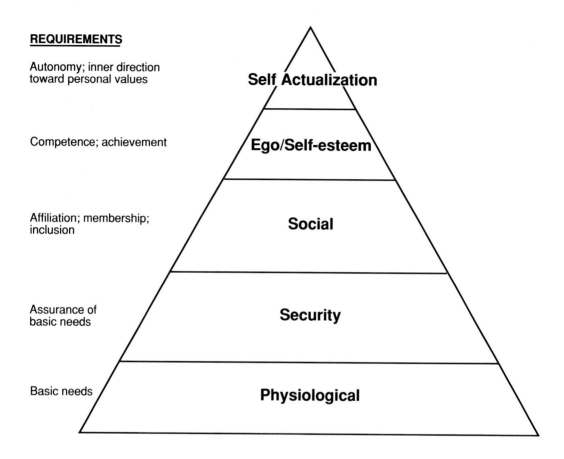

REQUIREMENTS

Autonomy; inner direction
toward personal values — Self Actualization

Competence; achievement — Ego/Self-esteem

Affiliation; membership;
inclusion — Social

Assurance of
basic needs — Security

Basic needs — Physiological

2.2 Maslow's Hierarchy of Human Needs

There are portions of any population that are chiefly preoccupied with a struggle to survive – to provide food, clothing, and shelter for themselves and their families. The Values and Lifestyles Segments index identifies these as Sustainers and Survivors. They are people whose incomes are irregular, or small and fixed. The intensely poor, the homeless, and some elderly fit into these groups. There is a clear ethical and moral responsibility for museums to seek to serve these audiences. Usually the approach must be done outside the museum walls, in the community at large. In the streets, in the schools, and through outreach programs Sustainers and Survivors can be affected. However, well-intended efforts to persuade people in desperate circumstances to spend time at the museum can have negative rather than positive results.

Maslow's hierarchical list of needs asserts that meeting basic requirements for sustaining human life must come before any person will have either the energy, will, or time to pursue cultural enrichment. History, art, and the sciences have little meaning when the here-and-now struggle to survive fully occupies one's attention.

On the other hand are the people who regularly come to the museum. They come often and require little in the way of enticement. The reasons for their interest in museums are varied, but such patrons are ordinarily fairly well educated and do not lack basic human resources. However, great wealth is by no means a given.

The segments between these two levels are where the museum audience challenge exists: the non-participants and occasional visitors. That challenge is to persuade people who have basic resources that the museum is a worthwhile, enriching, and even fun place to spend their leisure time.

The special circumstances of some segments of the population with special requirements may also suggest target audiences. For example, older citizens are a rapidly increasing segment of most societies and have their own concerns and prerequisites. Problems such as transportation limitations, the dislike for going places alone, reluctance to venture out at night, limited visual acuity, and feeling uncomfortable with unfamiliar situations influence visitation by senior citizens. People with visual, hearing, and mobility disabilities also have special needs and should be considered as target audiences too.

Museums are making efforts to serve all of these and other groups. Some endeavors include:

- tactile exhibits for persons with visual disabilities
- docent guided tours
- audiovisual devices
- day-time special activities
- transportation options
- exploration activities
- docents with sign-language capabilities
- emphasis on first-hand experience
- demonstrations

All of these are ways to afford special audiences effective and rewarding museum experiences.

The point is that various perceptions and circumstances combine to keep people away from museums. When targeting an audience, one must be sensitive to such concerns, work around the negatives, and meet needs positively and creatively. Such efforts will, in fact, improve the visit for everyone.

Motivations

People have reasons for choosing one type of leisure activity over another. Consciously or not, they are looking for certain kinds of places, people, or activities that meet personal criteria. Since individuals differ, the criteria differ. However, there are some commonly held motivations that humans focus on when deciding about pastimes. Marilyn Hood lists six criteria that adults use in making such choices.[3] They are:

- being with people, or social interaction
- doing something worthwhile
- having the challenge of new experiences
- having an opportunity to learn
- participating actively
- feeling comfortable and at ease in one's surroundings

Social needs probably play the largest role. Most museum visitors prefer to visit with a family member, a friend, or as part of a group.

The value of the visit, its challenges, and the educational opportunities provided are aspects of the design and content of the exhibition itself. These must be pre-planned and built into the presentations. Also, the interactive aspect of exhibitions relates to predetermined goals and execution. However, feeling comfortable is a broader matter. It involves the total museum experience for the visitor.

What kind of environment is a museum? Is it like a school, a library, a supermarket, an amusement park, or an arcade? Museums share characteristics with all of these, but perhaps the most significant aspect is informality. Even in what might be considered stodgy or stuffy museums, the informal nature of the experience is inescapable. There is no compulsion – no force allowed, needed, or wanted – in a museum visit. With the possible exception of school and guided tours, visitors can do as they wish within reason. They can learn at their own pace, in their own way, or not at all if they choose.

A patron will react negatively to an environment in which he or she is not physically or intellectually comfortable. If one feels uncomfortable then exit-oriented behavior or avoidance is probable. Comfort is an essential criterion for motivating people to visit museums. It demands that a museum provide its visitors with an informal, comfortable environment for a beneficial learning experience.

Comfort is the state of being at ease in one's surroundings and with the demands of the environment. Situations or circumstances that cause emotional or physical stress are uncomfortable. However, many pastimes involve a degree of physical discomfort. Playing games such as baseball, racquetball, soccer, or football can bring about a considerable level of physical distress. Participation in games of chance, volunteering to help those with disabilities, or even reading a book can cause emotional agitation. Yet, people will enthusiastically and repeatedly pursue even those leisure activities that involve profound discomfort.

This illustrates that there are acceptable and unacceptable forms of discomfort. There are those that people will avoid almost without exception. Most will select leisure activities that include positive interaction and involve very little fear of failure. Leisure activities need to create a sense of affirmation for the participant. Activities that engender feelings of inferiority, insecurity, intimidation, or embarrassment will be avoided. For many people, a museum is that kind of place. The facilities appear cold and formal, and the exhibitions are perceived as requiring a high level of education and extreme effort to grasp. No one enjoys feelings of inadequacy in understanding or appreciating the exhibitions presented for them.

In choosing an activity for breaks from daily labors, people will pick those that make them feel welcome, appreciated, provided for, and adequate – in short, places and activities that are enjoyable and worthwhile. Museums have come a long way in attempting to present an interesting, comfortable face to the public. However, wayfinders, information desks, air-conditioning, and friendly guards will not help if the visitor feels intimidated by the content and language of the exhibits. He or she will fear appearing foolish or dull-witted, and after spending a brief time will leave the museum, perhaps never to return.

It is a commonly held belief, by many museum professionals, that visitors do not read labels, will not look at objects, do not change their views or attitudes, and continually look for the exit. If such an attitude is found in museum staffs, how adequate can their efforts be to make exhibitions attractive to visitors? In fact, most visitors are looking for positive, meaningful experiences in museums. If they fail to find that sort of atmosphere, they may not be back.

Museum exhibitions ought to offer answers to the questions visitors want answered. Questions about how things work, how events occurred, and what people and the world were like long ago. Exhibitions offer the chance to look at and experience the "real thing." They arouse and satisfy curiosity, leading to continued and growing interests.

Learning and museum exhibitions

Satisfying expectations and stimulating curiosity bring people to museums and persuade them to return. Levels of visitor interest vary widely. The degree of success in capturing patrons' interest depends upon how well an exhibition catches their attention.

There are three basic types of museum visitor. There is overlap between these generalizations, and some people will exhibit one type of behavior at one time and in one museum, and another somewhere else. It can be helpful to look at these groupings as an intellectual exercise. They form a framework to think about the various levels of information that exhibitions need to present, because not every visitor looks at every part of an exhibition.

First, there are those people who move through a gallery quickly and display exit-oriented behavior. They are often casual visitors using their leisure time to participate in what they consider a worthwhile activity without becoming heavily involved. They may be persons with a psychological aversion to structured situations. Yet again, they may be persons who wish to be seen as appreciating "cultural" activities, but who do not truly appreciate the opportunities afforded them. Whatever the motivation, these people spend very little time closely examining exhibit objects or content.

The second group, on the other hand, are those who show a genuine interest in the museum experience and the collections. However, they ordinarily do not spend much time reading, especially texts that appear difficult or require too much effort to understand. These people prefer a casual, headline approach to information display. They respond strongly to situations that offer visual stimuli. The objects are the main focus of attention. Having absorbed what they consider to be adequate superficial information from an object, they move on in search of further stimulus. Occasionally, the cursory visitor will stop and examine something closely if it arouses sufficient curiosity and interest. This attention is sporadically and erratically given throughout the galleries.

The people in the third group are a minority. These are folks who will examine exhibitions with much more attention. They are willing, and usually able, to understand presented materials no matter how technical. They spend an abundance of time in the galleries, read the text and labels, and closely examine the objects. They are often frequent visitors to museums and require little enticement to come.

Why do some rush through exhibitions and others stroll or study? These behaviors have to do with how people are equipped to and prefer to gain knowledge. Training, prior experiences, and educational level affect the ease with which a person assimilates knowledge. However, it is the capability of exhibitions to capture visitor attention that most dramatically influences learning effectiveness. If attention is focused upon a subject, object, or activity, the chances are good that learning will take place.

Most people prefer active participation over passive observation. That is because, although humans are primarily visual creatures, the other senses reinforce what is gained by sight. For example, the visual aspects of a sculpture immediately elicit a desire to touch it. The touching reinforces, confirms, and adds to the information gained through the eyes. This is why museums, weighing the obligation to expose collections to public scrutiny against the responsibility to care for the objects, are often contradictory learning environments. "Do not touch" signs are psychologically offensive because they deny basic human learning behavior.

The way to address such conflicting missions lies with how humans gather, process, and store information. People have three principal means of gathering information, through:

- Words – language, both heard and read, requires the most effort and mental processing to extract meaning.
- Sensations – taste, touch, smell, hearing are more immediate and associative.
- Images – visual stimulus is the strongest, most memorable of the methods.

A large percentage of the information gathered by humans is visual. People process incoming images in six basic ways. These are:

- pattern seeking and recognition;

- mentally rotating objects in space;
- identifying dynamic structures, or mentally constructing movement capacities of objects;
- orthographic imagination or mentally constructing three-dimensional objects from two-dimensional representations such as maps or schematics;
- x-ray visualization or visualizing relationships as though one could see through objects;
- visual reasoning or imagining action/reaction events.

When an exhibition induces a person to engage in one or more of these mental operations, attention is arrested for a moment and interest is generated. Conroy of the Anniston Museum of Natural History suggests that people are affected by certain characteristics of objects:[4]

- larger objects produce longer viewing times
- moving objects produce longer viewing times
- novel or special objects attract more attention
- certain qualities of objects are more intrinsically interesting (e.g., dangerous objects, baby animals, valuable objects)

Although vision is the principal sense, what people perceive through whole-sensory experience is retained far better than that gained through sight alone. A person will remember more about what he or she does.

The solutions to exhibition design would be relatively simple if the only factors were those already mentioned. Those are aspects of the patron that, with some degree of thought and skill, can be affected with an anticipated level of success. However, there is at least one aspect of visitor psyche that is unpredictable from an exhibit design point of reference – worldview.

Design is dramatically affected by the perceptions of the visitor. No matter how clever the designer is and no matter how adroit the manipulation of learning factors, the patron's worldview will color every perception.

Worldview is a personal, cognitive (rational) structure or model of the world composed of how the person sees him- or herself, and how he or she views reality. A few of the factors that influence one's worldview are:

- culture
- religion
- physiology
- psychology
- socio-economic status
- race and ethnic background

The foundations for building the cognitive structure are:

- facts as they are perceived
- concepts, propositions
- theories, generalizations
- raw perceptual data

In fact, everything a person sees, feels, hears, touches, smells, or tastes has an effect on their worldview. Even if those influences are subconscious, they have very real effects on conscious thought.

One's worldview forms the filter through which incoming information is:

- evaluated (value judgments)
- anticipated (pre-judgments and prejudices)
- interpreted (processed for meaning)

Every visitor enters the museum with a personalized set of preconceived data and expectations. If what they encounter is unfamiliar or cannot be readily fitted to their worldview, they will be diffident and uncomfortable. Such reactions may effectively close the door on further communication. When confronted with an object with little interpretation, that is seemingly arbitrarily controversial, or one presented in a scholarly, technical manner, most visitors will avoid it and move on.

What, then, is the answer to the unpredictable nature of visitor reactions? In exhibit design, sensitivity to community attitudes, codes, conventions, and traditions must be part of the equation. An effective means of gaining a visitor's attention and cooperation is to preface an exhibition with something familiar and easily assimilated. If this is done, then new information can follow. When presented in easily digestible bits, virtually any degree of difficulty in subject matter can be addressed.

Recognizable activities (life cycles, everyday functions or objects) and human relationships (family, sibling rivalries, children, home activities, pets) are the kinds of subjects with which most people immediately identify and feel comfortable. Familiarity with an image or situation evokes memories. This leads to recognition, interest, curiosity, and subsequently, learning.

In addition to familiarity or recognition, an exhibition must provide a context or framework in which objects exist. Memories are stored as frameworks, patterns, and associations. Facts are not remembered for long as isolated units. When they are fitted into a framework of references, they form lasting impressions.

Also affecting the efficacy of learning is the physiology of the human brain, or brain function. The human brain is in reality two separate brains linked by way of a communication network. They are called the right and left brains, and their functions are different and complementary. Individuals learn in markedly differing manners depending upon the degree of dominance by one side or the other in their thought processes.

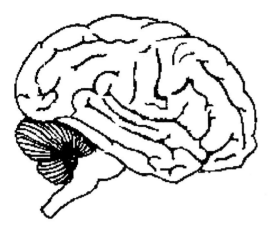 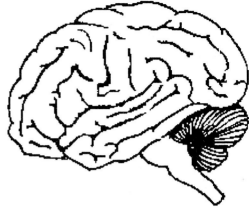

Right Brain	Left Brain
• Discerns integral understanding of complex patterns and structure–intuitive reasoning.	• Translates perceptions into logical, semantic, phonetic images.
• Responds to visual information.	• Communicates via logic-analytical thought-processing.
• Center of affective learning.	• Center of cognitive learning.
• Perceives the whole context (gestalt) from bits and pieces of information.	• Controls language, rational reasoning, reading, writing, counting and digital communication.
• Is appealed to directly through jokes, pictures, sounds, smells and touch.	• Understands and processes factual, concrete information.
• The "creative" side of the brain.	• The "logical" side of the brain.
• Understands humor and abstrac-tions. Dominates visual thinking.	• Usually the dominant side of the brain.

2.3 Functions of the brain

The left brain is normally dominant. This side:

- translates perceptions into logical, semantic, and phonetic images;
- communicates via logic-analytical processing;
- controls language and reasoning, reading, writing, counting, and digital communication.

The right brain acts in a more holistic manner. This half:

- discerns integral understanding of complex patterns and structures – intuition;
- perceives the whole context (gestalt) from bits and pieces;
- responds to images, not verbal language;
- contains a holistic worldview;
- is appealed to directly through jokes, pictures, sounds, smells, touch (cartoons are effective because of this).

Most formal education is organized around cognitive learning (meanings, functions, concepts, reasons, formulae, definitions). These are left brain activities. Schools in western cultures are structured with these rational functions. However, coupling left brain analysis with right brain imaging can promote faster, more rewarding, and more effective learning. By aiming exhibit design at a complementary employment of both sides of the brain, learning can be enhanced.

The right brain can draw associations from suggestions and fragmentary images. A cowboy hat or boots can evoke complex images of the American West into a storyline. The right brain allows one to provide a whole reality from a few pieces. This we call intuition. Therein also lies a danger since the conjured reality may be erroneously based on misconceived notions. Associations from the cowboy hat may lead one to formulate the false reality of the movie star image. This contradicts the true image of the hard-working, underpaid cowhand of history.

Museums offer real objects – the ideal diet for whole brain activity. Collections provide right brain appeal coupled with left brain cognition. This is why museums are vital alternative, complementary learning environments for schools and others who gain information primarily through spoken or printed material.

Conclusions

How can the above topics be integrated into an exhibition design methodology? Here are some suggestions:

- Museums are people places. They should make every effort to afford visitors with comfortable, rewarding experiences. Wayfinders, adequate facilities, and public-oriented exhibitions will help people feel that they belong and give them a sense of ownership.

- Examining the community is necessary. Museums must take the initiative to evaluate, identify, and actively pursue audiences previously overlooked.
- Exhibitions should capitalize on their strengths as places for personal encounters with collection objects. It is the appeal of the "real thing" that brings most people to museums.
- Imagery and exhibit elements that contain recognizable features, symbols, and associations will assist in audience retention. Rely upon community values and traditions to assist in gaining audience attention. Appeal to the human interest elements in images to gain visitor confidence in their own ability to understand the subject matter.
- Use strong visual impact to "hook" visitor curiosity. Bright colors, large graphics, varied shapes, and similar visual elements will attract a visitor's attention.
- Use graphics that tell stories and engage visitors in mental activities. Activate the visual/mental manipulative capability of the human brain by asking questions and providing demonstrations.
- Arrange objects in contextual settings. Provide a framework for objects that will assist the visitor in learning about them. Extend the framework along the storyline to lend continuity to the whole exhibition.
- Use sensory stimuli – sound, smell, touch, taste – to reinforce visual images. Whenever possible, use all the senses, but always try to involve at least two or three.
- Weave the cognitive, didactic elements of the storyline into the contextual framework and imagery of the whole exhibition.
- When writing text, labels, and audio narration, use language that evokes mental imagery. Without becoming trite or offensive, use word pictures instead of technical language.

3

Designing exhibitions

Designing museum exhibitions is the art and science of arranging the visual, spatial, and material elements of an environment into a composition that visitors move though. This is done to accomplish pre-established goals. The presentation of exhibitions in museums should never be haphazard or left to chance. Although planning can be overdone for almost any project, quality museum exhibitions require a high degree of development and design to serve the public properly. Design decisions should be deliberate and calculated, and executed to achieve maximum effect. Though a certain degree of serendipity plays a role, relying upon it too heavily is a mistake. A well-founded knowledge of design basics can foster an organized approach to exhibition design.

Certain elements of design are fundamental to all visual arts. An introduction to these elements is helpful in understanding why some arrangements work – that is, they fulfill their intended function – while others do not. When a composition works, it is usually comfortable to the eye, even if the subject matter may not be. However, when design fails, people will react negatively, regardless of how beautiful or important the contents are.

Naming the key elements of design varies, depending upon the person naming and their interests. However, there are six main elements. These are:

- value
- color
- texture
- balance
- line
- shape

Value

Value is the quality of lightness or darkness, having no reference specifically to color. Areas that are black have the lowest value; areas that are white, the highest. All the infinite stages between are varying degrees or shades of value.

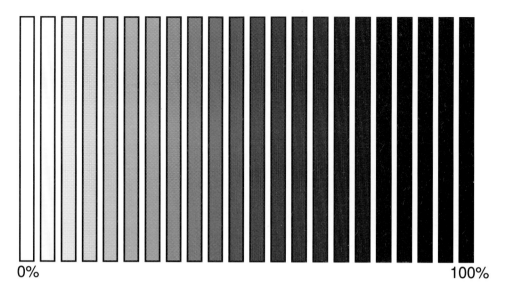

0%   100%

3.1 Value scale by 5 percent increments

Values are associated with visual weight characteristics. Normally, darker values are attributed the quality of heaviness; lighter shades are expressed as lighter in weight. For design purposes, values are important for emphasis, orientation, and attraction/repulsion. Judicious combining of value with the other design elements can dramatically affect the visual impact. Value is controlled by pigment, surface treatment, and lighting.

Color

Color is an extensive subject. To attempt to cover all aspects of color would be inappropriate in this context. However, addressing basic principles is fitting. Few substances are entirely without color. Some may appear colorless or mono-chromatic, but all influence light in some way. Color requires both the physical characteristics of light energy and the action of the human brain. Colors are perceived through the filter of perception and are ascribed meanings.

Consider the physical properties of color. Light is a form of electromagnetic energy or radiation, the result of applying energy to a substance like a tungsten filament, a candle, or a fluorescent gas. In all cases, the consequence of energizing the materials is the emission of waves/particles called photons. We call this light. The speed at which the photons travel or vibrate is referred to as their frequency. There are an infinite number of frequencies, but the human eye recognizes only a small band. This narrow collection of frequencies is known as the visible light spectrum (VLS), or simply visible light. Above and below the visible band are frequencies of radiation we know as heat, ultraviolet, radio, microwave, and many others.

33

Light travels through space basically in a straight line from its source until it reaches an obstruction – like an object. All substances influence the energy that reaches them. Light that reaches the eye affects the receptors in the retina directly. Light that reaches another object first, then finds its way to the eye, may undergo several changes in direction and speed. Light triggers visual sensors in the retina of the eyeball. These generate a series of messages that are sent through the optic nerve to the visual centers of the brain. There the signals are given a name – a color.

There are several energy changes that substances may cause when light strikes them. In most cases, more than one form of energy transaction takes place. Photons are reflected from a surface, transmitted through a material, refracted by having the wavelengths split and redirected, or absorbed and changed into heat or chemical energy. The whole process of reflection, refraction, transmission, and absorption dictates what wavelengths of light reach the retina, thus determining the colors perceived.

Colors have many characteristics. Various substances are known to produce a desired color consistently. We call them pigments. Some pigments are naturally occurring while others are artificial in origin. However, the basis of all pigment-produced colors is three primary colors – red, yellow, and blue. By mixing the primaries, all other colors are produced.

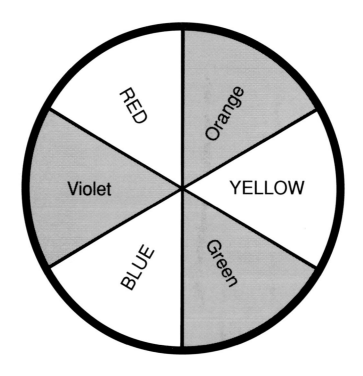

3.2 Basic color wheel

Excepting black and white, mixing pigments produces increasingly muddy colors. This is a process of increasing the absorptive properties of the pigment mix. When virtually all frequencies of the light are absorbed, little or none of it arrives at the eye, resulting in perceived blackness. White is at the other end of the pigment scale. It is a pigment that reflects and mixes all wavelengths.

Direct methods of stimulating vision with lighting devices seem to contradict the previous statements. Mixing all wavelengths of color produces white. Actually, the same process is operating. Mixing all wavelengths of light together is the same as reflecting them all. The resulting mixture is what we perceive as white.

On the other hand, as with total absorption, when all wavelengths are prevented from reaching the eye, the result is blackness. The lights go out.

No matter how light energy is produced or how it is affected by objects, the human brain is the interpreter. Characteristics attributed to color relate to associations. The colors from the yellow middle of the visible spectrum to red are "warm." This is probably because the radiation frequencies below red in the spectrum are sensed as heat. At the other end, toward blue, the colors are referred to as "cool." This end is most distant from heat. It is associated with the coolness and blueness of the sky, ice, water, and other naturally cool substances and conditions.

Other characterizations are cultural, varying broadly depending upon the worldview of an individual. In this century, pink and blue signify female and male gender, respectively. However, a century ago in the United States, the reverse was true. White may stand for purity in one culture, grief or death in another, and magical properties in yet another. Black, red, green, and many other colors have cultural meanings as well. Some are quite complex. Color-induced meanings are usually laden with emotional impact. In language colors signify emotions, too. Blue means sadness or depression, green represents envy, and red signifies anger. Cultures vary in these kinds of associations as well.

Texture

Texture is the visual roughness or smoothness of a surface. In two-dimensional images no actual surface variations may exist, yet by varying the density of pigments, quality of line, and strength or weakness of values, the surface may appear to have a "toothiness." Texture may also result from the actual treatment of a surface and have a tactile dimension as well.

smoother ←————————————————————→ **rougher**

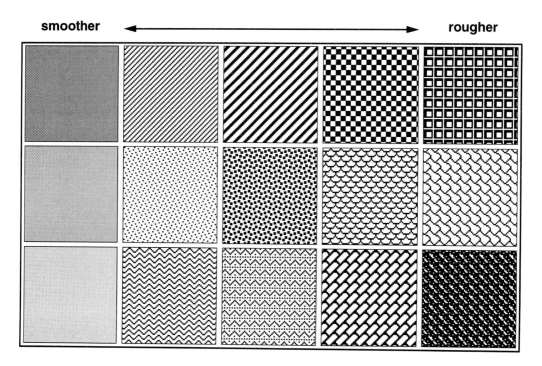

3.3 Illustrations of visual textures

Balance

Balance is the quality of visual weight distribution. When images or objects are arranged symmetrically – items of equal size and weight match across a mid-point – they are in symmetrical balance. When they are arranged so no equivalents exist, the composition is asymmetrical. Balance can be either formal or informal. Between symmetry and asymmetry are infinite variations of balance. Typically, symmetry is formal composition. On the other hand, asymmetry is informal.

Balance does not always employ object balanced against object. Another way is to balance an object (a positive element) against a non-object (a negative element – space). Adept use of negative space can dramatically enhance the visual interest of a composition, while producing a comfortable balance.

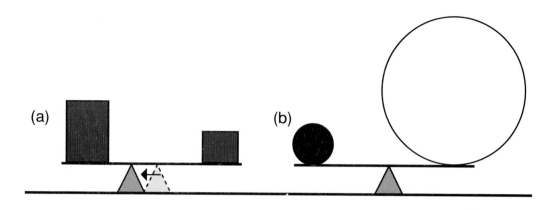

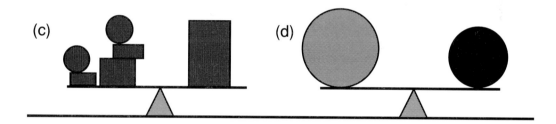

3.4 Visual balance achieved by:
   (a) shifting the center of balance
   (b) use of negative space
   (c) employing multiple versus single elements
   (d) offsetting values and volumes

Line

Line is the quality of linearity. A line is a string of points with little or no space between them and next to each other to lead the eye and thus suggest direction. Line gives a strong directional content to composition. It can vary in strength, density, width, and other qualities. These impart characteristics, add textural qualities, affect visual weight, imply directionality, show containment, and delineate space.

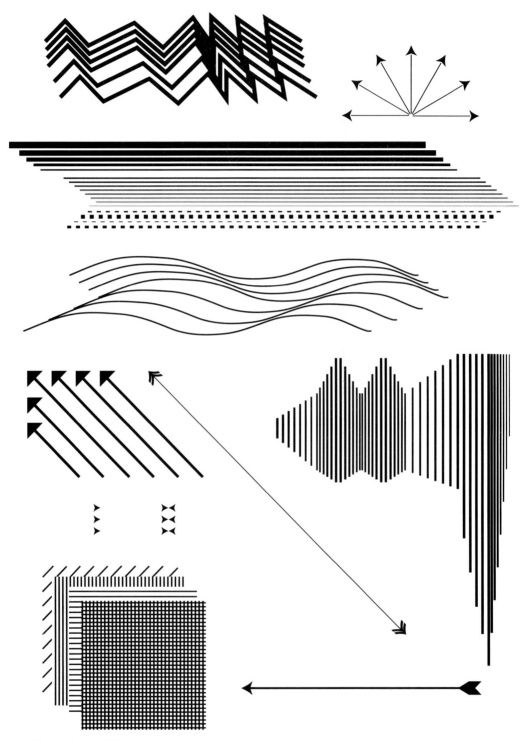

3.5 Illustrations of line

Shape

Shape is the element of physical or spatial containment. It is the composite of all points forming the internal or external surface of a composition. Both two- and three-dimensional shapes are everywhere and infinite in variety. Some are geometrical and hard-edged, like squares, cubes, rectangles, triangles, circles, and cylinders. Others are softer, more curvilinear, as are living organisms. These are called organic shapes. Contrasting, joining, overlapping, and mixing shapes adds important visual interest to any composition. The juxtaposition of organic and geometric shapes can accentuate the qualities of both.

These design elements can be expanded upon much more. There are ample references that can provide further information. The essential properties of each element need to be understood by the designer. By using both experimental and traditional combinations of the design elements, compositions are built. Careful thought will produce useful designs, but intuitive leaps of imagination often inspire the most exceptional compositions. The keys are to experiment and observe.

Human factors in exhibition design

The human being is a design factor that influences and relates to all other composition-related considerations. Fundamentally, human beings have only one archetype with minor variations in size, weight, features, and the like. The basic model includes a main section (trunk), appendages (arms and legs) and a head. These are symmetrically organized along the mid-line of a spinal column. Variations in girth, height, length of foot, and hat-size are relatively minor, no matter how important they may be to a person's self-image. The largest variations in size exist between youth and adulthood. There is roughly a 162 percent increase in height from age 5 to 20. In contrast, the difference in average height between adult males and females is less than 1 percent. Most people fit into the chart on p. 41. Those persons with special needs add other dimensions to the data. General measurements have been provided for persons in wheelchairs, since these devices add significantly to a person's spatial requirements.

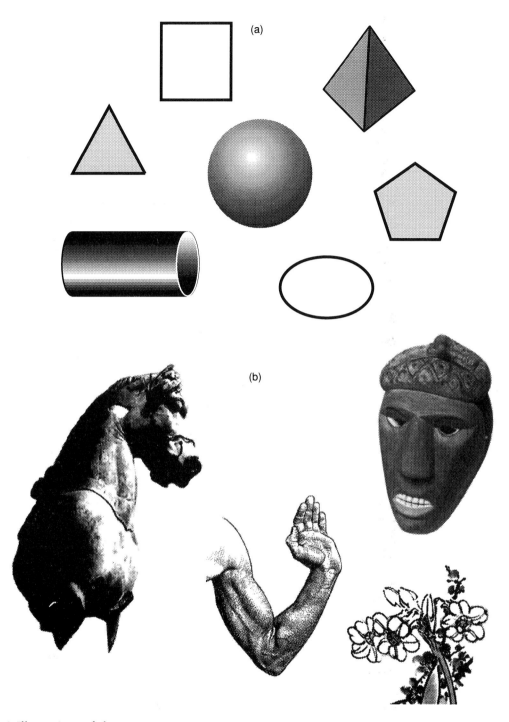

3.6 Illustrations of shape
  (a) Geometric shapes
  (b) Organic shapes

Standard human dimensions

Criteria	Female	Male	Child at age 8
standing height	64.5 inches (163.8cm)	70 inches (177.8cm)	51 inches (129.5cm)
eye-level standing	60 inches (152.4cm)	66 inches (167.6cm)	48 inches (121.9cm)
shoulder width	20 inches (50.8cm)	20 inches (50.8cm)	12 inches (30.5cm)
arms extended forward	33 inches (83.8cm)	36 inches (91.4cm)	25.5 inches (64.8cm)
arms extended upward	80.5 inches (204.5cm)	89.5 inches (227.3cm)	63 inches (160cm)
arms extended to sides	66 inches (167.6cm)	72 inches (182.9cm)	60 inches (152.4cm)
turning radius	48 inches (121.9cm)	48 inches (121.9cm)	36 inches (91.4cm)
seat height	15 inches (38.1cm)	18 inches (45.7cm)	13 inches (33cm)
wheelchair width	25 inches (63.5cm)	25 inches (63.5cm)	25 inches (63.5cm)
wheelchair length	42.5 inches (108cm)	42.5 inches (108cm)	42.5 inches (108cm)
eye-level from wheelchair	44 inches (111.8cm)	49 inches (124.5cm)	36 inches (91.4cm)

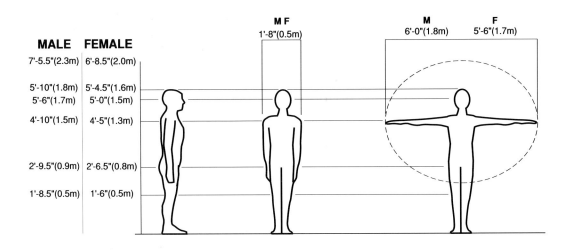

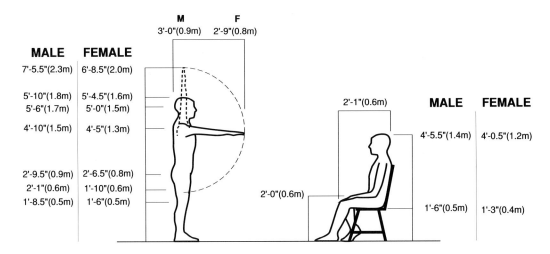

3.7 Basic human dimensions (adult)

What do these human dimensions tell the designer about involving people in learning experiences? People feel most at ease in spaces that allow freedom of movement without feeling either overly confined or exposed. This relates to a sense of scale – human scale. We relate space to ourselves as the fixed unit of measurement. Ceiling heights in most homes are between 9 and 12 ft, providing space to raise our arms above our heads, but low enough to feel comfortable. Spaces intended to be impressive or awe-inspiring are normally much larger and higher. Think of places such as churches, cathedrals, banks, public buildings, and business centers. The larger the space, the smaller the individual appears by contrast. Being lost in a vast space carries the emotional sensation of being less able to control the environment. The less control a person has, the more impressive, awe-inspiring the space becomes.

On the other hand, spaces that are small and tight engender crowded, oppressive, smothering feelings. Many people have negative associations with such responses. The minimum comfortable space is defined by the room to swing one's arms outstretched side to side. The significance and usefulness of this factor in exhibit design vary depending upon the intended impact of the space. An intimate exhibition requires less room than does a grandiose one.

The implications of human response to space and the means by which we gather information become clearer as they relate to behavioral tendencies. Some of these behaviors are familiar to designers and have developed into some practical guidelines.

Touching

People have an innate predisposition for touching, both as a sensory and experiential confirmation of what they see, and as memory reinforcement. If objects or surfaces are within reach, they will be touched. Erecting barriers to separate the viewer physically from the object is possible, of course. However, this is sometimes undesirable for design reasons. Spatial separation can protect without creating resentment. If the objects are out of reach, they are outside the touch behavior. Younger children have not learned the social conventions and must be physically prevented from touching to ensure collection safety.

Entry response

People will normally use the largest opening when presented with a choice, and all other factors are roughly equal. This is entry response. When entering a new and largely unknown space, larger and well lit is better. It is less intimidating and leaves more room for exploring what is ahead.

Viewing height

People are most comfortable and will spend more time looking and reading when printed materials and objects are comfortably placed. They should be positioned so the center of the material is at eye-level. For adults, average height is around 5 ft 3 in (1.6 m). The field of vision forms a cone beginning at the eyes and extending 40° above and below the horizontal axis. Distance from the object increases or decreases the comfortable viewing area within the cone. Placing objects or graphics outside the cone leads to difficulty in viewing and fatigue. The space outside the cone of vision can be used for large, bold elements, but should be avoided for detailed ones.

(a) Barricade and vitrine

(b) Implied. *Trough with branch* by Sara Waters

(c) Barricade

(d) Ropes

3.8 Barriers, ropes, and implied boundaries. Barriers may be actual or implied, purchased or constructed. Their purpose is to protect the objects and the visitors from each other. However, they should not interfere with a visitor's ability to see the exhibit, or detract unnecessarily from the object's aesthetic qualities.

3.9 Gallery entrances. The entrance to a gallery sets the tone and mood for an exhibition. It lets the visitor know what to expect. The entry also establishes the traffic pattern for the gallery.

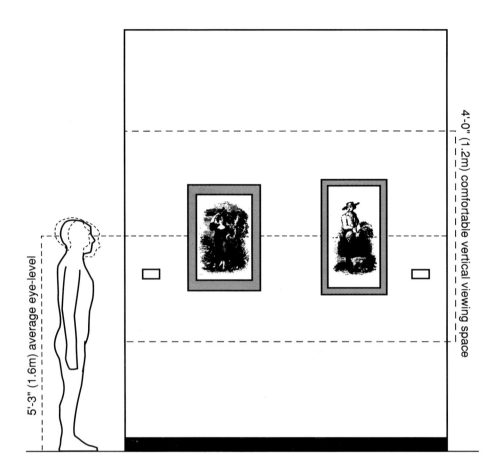

3.10 Viewing height and comfortable visual space

Sitting or leaning

People will sit on any surface that is at or near a comfortable height, and close to horizontal. If anything is a suitable height, people will prop their feet on it or lean on it. These actions are automatic and without thought, often in response to fatigue.

Space, as perceived by humans, has emotional associations as well as physical ones. Various kinds of space evoke suitable and largely predictable emotional responses. This can be helpful in design. For instance, to promote the close viewing of small objects, a space that is smaller, more dimly lit, and in which important objects are highlighted invites scrutiny and stimulates curiosity. A small object in a large hall may appear insignificant. The same object in a more intimate space becomes important and focal. The reverse is also true, and all the variations between have proper applications depending on the objects displayed.

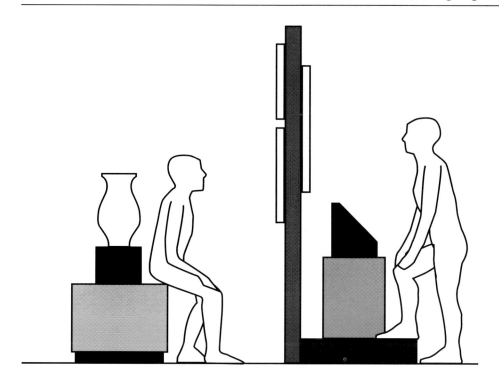

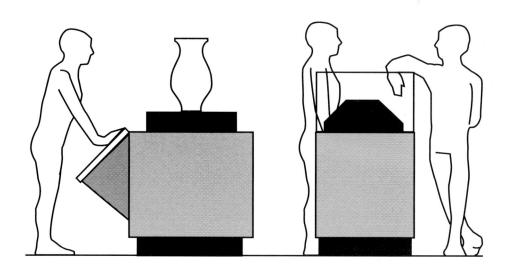

3.11 Sitting and leaning behavior

(a)

(b)

3.12 Spatial relationships
 (a) Cool and formal
 (b) Intimate and warm
 High ceilings, uniform flooring, general lighting, and light-colored wall treatments impart an impression of cool formality to a gallery. Lowered ceiling and textured flooring, along with low, directed lighting, lend a space a feeling of intimacy and warmth.

We can say that space may be defined in terms of the emotional responses aroused, as below:

- formal or informal
- cold or warm
- masculine or feminine
- public or private
- awesome or intimate
- graceful or vulgar

Not only do people react to the space around them, but also each carries a sense of space with him or her as an extension of the body and psyche. There are discernible behaviors associated with this portable space.

Personal space

Personal space is delineated by the span of one's reach, and is a reaction to the approach of persons outside one's intimates. Although a friend, family member, or spouse may be allowed within one's personal space, strangers and acquaintances are expected to keep a proper distance. In some societies, this space may be more compact than in others through necessity. This is seen in persons from crowded metropolitan areas. However, when personal space is perceived as violated, an individual will react either to repel or to move away from the offender. Both responses create discomfort and negative feelings. Applying this principle in a gallery context means giving visitors enough room to maintain their personal space when around others viewing the same exhibit.

Another form of space is territorial. Territorial space is a three-dimensional area over which an individual exercises control, such as an office or bedroom.

A primary form of spatial relationship is transactional space. This is where people carry on varied activities while in the presence of each other. Within transactional space are a set of sub-spaces delineated by the kinds of activities that occur in them. They are:

- distributional spaces
- collecting spaces
- transitional spaces

Areas where people enter and exit on the way to other places are distributional spaces. Places like corridors and lobbies are distributional in nature.

Rooms or areas where people gather or meet for a common purpose are collecting spaces. Examples are classrooms and auditoriums.

Transitional spaces are those through which people move from one place to another, such as atria and doorways.

Transactional spaces are common in museums and thus are important to the designer. Recognizing the nature of an area helps in planning with or around its inherent characteristics.

(a)

(b)

(c)

3.13 Illustrations of spaces
  (a) Collection spaces
  (b) Distributional space
  (c) Transitional spaces
Theaters and classrooms are collecting places. Lobbies and hallways are distributional spaces. Vestibules and entryways act as transitional areas to facilitate movement from one kind of space to another.

Behavioral tendencies

Among human beings there are shared behavioral tendencies. In some cases, typical behavior is modified by cultural or societal preferences. To create effects, move people, and attract attention it is normally wiser to play upon natural tendencies, rather than oppose them. Some of these shared behaviors are discussed in the following descriptions.

> **"A long standing observation, at least in the United States, is the marked tendency for people to turn to the right when entering an open or unstructured area."**[1]

- *Turning to the right*
  Most people tend to favor turning to the right if all other factors are equal. A possible explanation is that this relates to the dominance of right-handedness in humans.
- *Following the right wall*
  Once moving to the right, most people will stay to the right, leaving exhibits on the left less viewed.
- *Stopping at the first exhibit on the right side*
  The first exhibit area on the right gets the most attention. Conversely, the first one on the left gets less notice.
- *Stopping at the first exhibit rather than the last*
  Due to fatigue and the nearness of an exit, more interest is concentrated at the beginning of an exhibition than at the end.
- *Exhibits closest to exits are least viewed*
  The closer people are to an exit, the more they are drawn to it, and the less attention is given to the exhibits.
- *Preference for visible exits*
  Perhaps this behavior is a result of a subconscious desire to avoid traps. It is expressed as a reluctance to enter an area without visible exits.
- *Shortest route preference*
  Exhibits along the shortest route to the exit receive the largest amount of attention.
- *Lining up furniture around edges of rooms*
  Particularly in western cultures this is a tendency, though not a rule. Most often the center of the room is left as a transactional area. Oriental cultures tend to focus more on the center of the room.
- *Square corners preference*
  Western cultures typically build with corners and angles rather than curves.
- *Preference for right-angles and 45° angles*
  Most western cultures arrange walls and furniture at 90° or 45° angles to each other.

- *Reading from left to right, top to bottom*
  This is a language-dependent phenomenon. Asian languages often reverse or even overturn this convention. In western languages, right to left, top to bottom is a normal progression for viewing any object or graphic.
- *Aversion to darkness*
  Humans lack the acute night vision of many species. We are typically daylight creatures. Due to the inability to determine the contents and sizes in the dark, people avoid such places. Fear of the unknown as a survival reflex is probably the root motivation.
- *Chromaphilic behavior*
  Bright colors are visually engaging to most people. Although a person may not prefer bright hues, their eyes are drawn to the more brightly colored object or area.
- *Megaphilic behavior*
  Similar to chromaphilia, largeness is visually stimulating. People react first to larger objects when they enter a space.
- *Photophilic behavior*
  Also related to chromaphilia, most people react more positively toward areas of brighter illumination. This is probably linked to avoidance of darkness.
- *Exhibit fatigue*
  Mental and physical over-stimulation or over-exertion creates a common condition called exhibit fatigue.
- *Thirty-minute limit*
  The average maximum attention span for an adult audience is thirty minutes.
- *Larger type is read more*
  The larger and bolder the type graphically, the more attention it attracts. Conversely, areas of smaller text appear difficult, too technical, and are usually passed over.

Methodologies and design strategies

All the tendencies, attitudes, and responses addressed so far have a definite impact upon the design process. Ways of using this knowledge suggest themselves. If a gallery is not constructed in a way that permits normal tendencies and responses to occur, they must be compensated by alternative behavior. In other instances, playing upon the normal responses can enhance an otherwise mundane experience. Some suggestions for using this knowledge are:

- *Left turning upon entry*
  By creating an attractive, larger, brighter opening to the left, or by placing a barrier to force flow to the left, a designer can select against the right turning tendency.
- *See-through panels, exhibit cases, and windows*
  By using these devices, a designer can capture attention, draw visitors into

the next area, heighten mystery, create openness, and promote interest and movement.

- *Pools of light and color*
  Using areas of light and color as accents plays upon chromaphilic and photophilic tendencies, enticing visitors along a path of progression.
- *Landmark exhibits*
  Placing striking exhibits periodically throughout a gallery draws visitors through the gallery.
- *Use headlining and large type*
  These permit quick transfer of basic information such as themes, subdivisions, and topics. Headlines are visually more attractive than text blocks and are more often read.
- *Use diagonals and curves*
  The human eye follows lines. Diagonals and curves are visually active. They can lead people along, and achieve enough visual motion to allow a visitor to leave one exhibit and move to the next one.
- *Transitional spaces*
  Changes in ceiling height, color scheme, lighting level, aisle width, and other visual and physical manipulations promote shifts in attention, generate curiosity about the next space, and evoke emotional responses. Dim lighting promotes quietness and is calming. It can serve to ease the transition from one type of space to another.

Traffic flow approaches

Along with the design principles discussed, one additional factor should be addressed: the manner in which a visitor approaches the exhibition. The following three methods are fundamental. Depending upon the exhibition concept and educational objectives, each approach has advantages and disadvantages. Depending upon the approach chosen, designers can employ all their skills to effect the desired results. Variations are certainly possible, although the three listed are reasonably inclusive.

Suggested approach

This method uses colors, lighting, wayfinders, headlines, landmark exhibits, and similar visuals to draw visitors along a pre-chosen route without setting physical barriers to constrict movement into a single path. Perhaps the most challenging and difficult approach, it promotes a comfortable learning experience for the visitor by allowing freedom of choice while maintaining contextual continuity.

- Advantages – the suggested method provides a casual path for the patron while presenting information within a coherent framework and in digestible interpretive increments.
- Disadvantages – this method depends heavily upon the success of design elements to lead the learning experience.

53

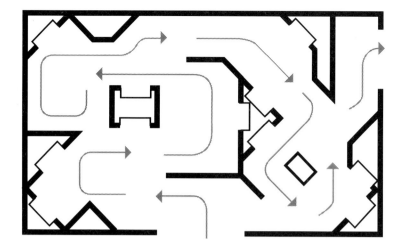

3.14 Floorplan of suggested approach to traffic flow

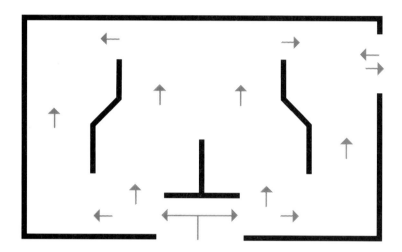

3.15 Floorplan of unstructured approach to traffic flow

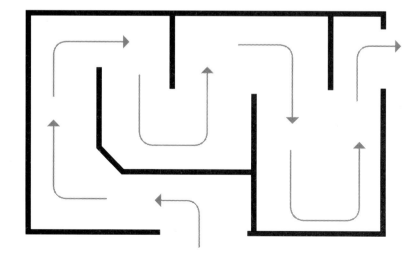

3.16 Floorplan of directed approach to traffic flow

Unstructured approach

Upon entering a gallery, a person may choose his or her own path without a suggested route that is right or wrong. Essentially, movement is non-directed and random. This method is often characteristic of art galleries.

● Advantages – this is a suitable approach for strongly object-oriented exhibitions. It allows visitors to move at their own pace and decide their own priorities. Interpretive material must be object-directed and not dependent upon a progressive format.
● Disadvantages – this approach does not work well with storylines or directional presentations.

Directed approach

This method is more rigid and restricted than the others. The gallery is normally arranged in a one-way traffic flow with minimal opportunities for exiting before the whole exhibition has been viewed.

● Advantages – this approach allows a very structured, coherent, and didactically oriented development of a subject.
● Disadvantages – this method often promotes exit-oriented behavior as the visitor looks for a way to leave the pathway. In some cases a sense of entrapment results, while in other instances it can lead to bottlenecks in traffic flow when one person wants to stroll through and study, and another wants to find the exit.

Object arrangement

Objects from the collections and other sources are the principal ingredient in most museum exhibitions. The arrangement of objects is of primary concern for the designer. Even as a designer manipulates space to strengthen a viewer's ability to perceive and assimilate exhibit content, so too objects must be organized to increase the impact and to emphasize the importance of each item. Their placement in relation to the visitor, the environment, and each other determines whether or not they will attract and hold the attention of the viewer.

There are two sorts of objects that the exhibit-maker deals with: those that are flat or two-dimensional, and those that have depth or are three-dimensional. Two-dimensional items are usually objects that are affixed to flat surfaces. Paintings, prints, drawings, posters, and some textiles are included under this heading. Although they do have some thickness, their visual importance is in only two planes. Three-dimensional objects, on the other hand, have noticeable depth and protrude into all the three dimensions: length, width, and depth.

Generally speaking, two-dimensional objects are hung on walls, or laid upon inclined surfaces or on the floor. Three-dimensional objects occupy sufficient space to be factors in the movement of people within a gallery. The distinction can be clarified by comparing a painting to a free-standing sculpture. Regardless of dimensional qualities, all objects have certain intrinsic visual characteristics that affect how they may be arranged. These are:

- *Visual impact*

  This refers to the characteristics of the object that arrest and hold attention and relates to the strength of the individual objects and to the whole. Color, directionality, texture, and other design elements work together to create the visual power of an object as perceived by the viewer. Monochromatic groupings depend heavily upon value, texture, visual mass, and weight. Color compositions depend upon these elements but add color relationships. It is important, however, that colors in objects do not compete to the detriment of one or more of the items. There are no hard and fast rules since design depends upon the intent of the designer and the desired impact.

- *Visual weight*

  The values, textures, colors, and other design elements combine to imbue the overall composition with the quality of weightedness. For example, a painting with a large amount of light color depicting sky will give the impression of lightness and openness. One with somber tones and dark colors will appear heavier and more ponderous.

- *Visual direction*

  Many objects have a quality that leads the eyes of the viewer in a direction – directionality. Linear elements, color sequences, weight distributions, and other design factors affect the directionality of an object or composition.

- *Visual balance*

  Visual weight, color, and directionality combine to give an object the quality of balance. Imbalance is visually unsettling, giving the impression of being in motion or leaning. Balance produces the feeling of being at rest.

- *Visual mass*

  Objects have the visual quality of solidity or opacity. Color, texture, value, and linearity all lend the object this quality. The visual mass relates to the apparent density of an object.

Museums deal with paintings, photographs, prints or drawings, and many other flat objects such as textiles, posters, and tapestries. The overall arrangement of such objects is important in attracting and holding attention, leading the eye to focal points, and creating a comfortable visual experience. Granted, comfort is not always the intent of the designer, and there are instances where discomfort related to subject matter may be desirable. However, providing conditions conducive to learning means achieving visual coherence in most situations.

When arranging flat objects on a vertical surface such as a panel or gallery wall, the rule of thumb is to place the items at a comfortable viewing height. The accepted average eye-level for adults is 5 ft 3 in (1.6 m). Usually, this means placing the visual mass of the objects so the viewing height coincides with the vertical center of the objects.

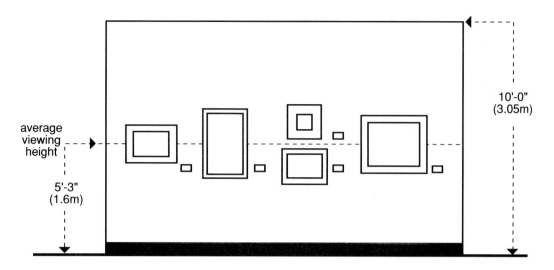

3.17 Viewing height and center of mass

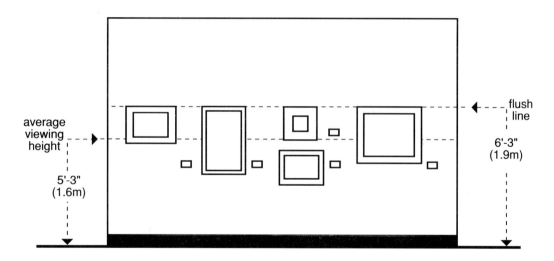

3.18 Flush arrangement

Center line alignment gives an arrangement of several flat pieces of differing sizes a visually balanced relationship. Even with grouped works where one is placed above the other, the center line will pass through the middle of the total visual mass.

Another less useful arrangement is the flush alignment. Objects are arranged so all the top or bottom edges align. The center line/eye-level relationship is lost in this organization.

This arrangement does not work well except in special instances. It appears an unnatural or contrived concession to the physical environment.

In organizing objects along an eye-level center line, several characteristics of the objects themselves affect the placement.

Horizon lines

Particularly in representational works of art, part of the composition of the work is the implied viewpoint or eye-level of the viewer. This is the horizon line and it corresponds to the illustrated point where sky and earth meet. Horizon lines in varied works are often not in agreement with one another. Care should be exercised in placing paintings with incompatible horizon lines near each other. They can conflict and create visual imbalance, drawing more attention to their dissimilarities than to their individual merits.

Directionality

The direction in which an image leads the eyes – directionality – should be compatible with the intent of the designer. Some objects are strongly directional in appearance. The arrangement of groups of objects should strive to keep the viewer's eyes moving back into the overall composition. Some objects are self-contained in this respect. Others will decidedly lead the viewer's direction of view somewhere else. By combining the directional qualities of several objects, composition that enhances each piece can be achieved.

Balance

Balance is usually the desired result for arrangements of objects. The characteristics of individual objects should be balanced in relation to the whole. Placing dark paintings on one side and light paintings on the other will cause a visual imbalance. At times, proper use of negative space can be substituted for positive elements to create balance. It requires a proportionally larger amount of negative space to offset even a small object. Negative space that is too large simply becomes space and no longer serves to balance but becomes the background.

The above principles are true of any arrangement of objects, whether displayed as individual pieces or as groups of items. Grouping objects into cohesive and effective units is an art in itself. The overall composition of a grouping can profoundly affect the attention given to any object within it.

high horizon

middle horizon

low horizon

3.19 Horizon line arrangements

(a)

(b)

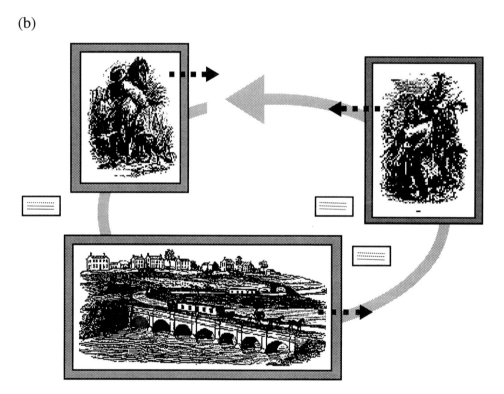

3.20 Directionality
(a) Directionality leading the eye away from the grouping, creating distraction and visual discomfort.
(b) The use of directionality to lead the viewer's eye around the grouping, helping to maintain visual interest and comfort.

Flanking

Flanking uses opposing elements to balance each other along a horizontal line, forcing the eyes toward the center of the grouping.

This method can employ either formal or informal balance, symmetry or asymmetry. The main distinction is that of opposing visual forces balanced across an imaginary pivot point.

Spiraling

Spiraling is more dynamic and uses the directional qualities of the objects to create a spiraling pattern of eye movement around the center of the visual mass.

Three-dimensional objects use the same rules and factors with the added dimension of depth. Depth allows very interesting and intricate relationships between objects to be established. As with flat items, individual three-dimensional objects are treated differently from groups of such objects. Isolating an object, whether flat or three-dimensional, confers importance to it, heightens drama, and emphasizes it. Care is needed in grouping three-dimensional objects to ensure each piece a proper amount of importance and attention.

To the factors mentioned, three-dimensional considerations add the relational aspect. This refers to the positioning of objects with respect to each other in the third dimension – depth. Objects placed in depth overlap from certain points of view and not from others. This position-dependent overlapping creates an infinite variety of relationships, adding interest to grouped objects. Overlapping in a horizontal plane means placing objects in front of each other. Overlapping in a vertical plane means the same from the vertical point of view. The movement of the viewer around a relational grouping causes an intricate interplay between the placement of objects, the point of view of the viewer, and the movement of the eyes. Orienting objects with each other so the viewer's focus of attention will remain within the grouping is a form of spiraling.

All of these principles and rules-of-thumb are only guidelines. They do not and can not supersede the well-trained eye of a designer. In the end, judgments about the proper relationships of objects to each other, to the room, and to the viewer are only based upon experience and an inner "feel" for the arrangement of things. However, by being aware of the principles, one can begin to build an experiential base from which to grow.

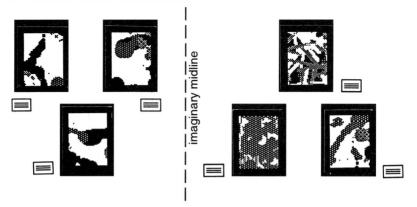

3.21 Balanced object arrangement

Special considerations

Going beyond designing for the "normal" person is an imperative in museums today. Populations are in constant flux and what might have been perceived as adequately accessible a few years ago is no longer acceptable. Important audiences can be overlooked or excluded if accessibility is not addressed in every exhibition. In some cases, exhibitions should be planned to address special needs for persons with visual, hearing, movement, or mental disabilities. Usually, special needs can be addressed in all exhibition designs. This normally has the effect of improving the museum experience for everyone. See p. 63 for considerations for designers about accessibility.

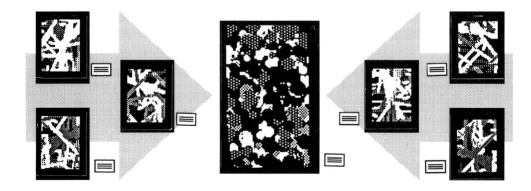

3.22 Flanking object arrangement

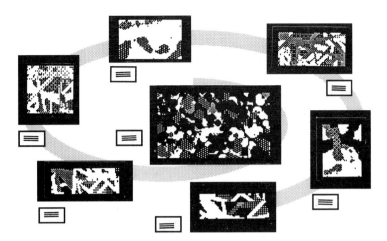

3.23 Spiraling object arrangement

- Adequate space for persons in wheelchairs to move comfortably. This includes not only exhibition galleries, but also building entries and exits, restrooms, food service areas, orientation spaces and assembly rooms, etc. – in essence, all areas of the museum building.
- Providing a variety of information channels so persons with hearing or visual disabilities can participate is important. The use of audio devices, high-contrast detailed photographs, close-captioned videos, interactive devices, touchable resources, and similar audiovisuals are all viable and valuable devices for sending information to all visitors, thereby enriching the learning experience.
- Including rest areas in gallery spaces helps to offset fatigue and provides necessary stops for the elderly, children, and those with mobility disabilities. In addition, such stops allow everyone a place for contemplation and reflection.
- Plan wayfinding clues inside and outside the museum. Clear, highly visible wayfinders are a principal method of welcoming visitors to your building. People dislike feeling lost or out of place. Wayfinders inspire confidence in the novice visitor and improve the experience. They can be in the form of signage, information persons strategically and conspicuously located, kiosks and electronic aids, or directional clues built into the exhibit design. When people can easily locate restrooms, places to sit down, or to get a drink, they are more comfortable, and so enjoy their visit. This puts them in a receptive frame of mind for learning and helps ensure that they will return to the museum.
- Meeting safety codes is a major item in any design. Providing adequate identification for fire exits does not always mean a glaring red sign. It does mean providing emergency lighting and adequate exits for emergency evacuation. Balconies with sturdy railings, appropriate protection for artifacts, lack of obstacles, and similar considerations are comforting for those with children or persons with disabilities.

These suggestions are certainly not exhaustive, but they do deal with some of the most pressing needs. There are many resources available to aid museums in meeting accessibility and safety requirements. The most important point is that such requirements should not be viewed as restrictive or punitive, but rather as opportunities to improve the quality of the museum experience for all visitors.

Presenting design ideas

In the process of designing and planning exhibitions, there is a need to communicate one's ideas to others. In the museum exhibition process, seldom is one able to plan and execute entirely without assistance or input. Since one of the primary tenets of exhibitry is that exhibitions are collective creative activities, communication between collaborators is essential, and not only between collaborators, but also with those who control the time, tools, materials, or the purse strings.

Perhaps the oldest human method of communicating ideas is by drawing pictures. This is the first step in exchanging ideas in the exhibit context. Floorplans, elevations, mechanical drawings, color sketches, renderings, and other graphics all give the uninitiated person visual clues about the designer's thoughts.

Models go one step further by providing the dimension of depth to the visual equation. Many people do not visualize well when viewing drawings. To some, a wall on a floorplan or blueprint may represent nothing more than a line. A model will extrude that line into a wall with height, length, and thickness.

At some point, the ideas described in the two- and three-dimensional representations must translate into a presentation which the creator makes to an administrator or donor. This is a formal presentation.

Most modern buildings come equipped with sets of blueprints. These are the drawings that the construction contractor used to build the facility. Often following completion of the building, a set of blueprints called "as-builts" are produced. These include changes made during construction and may more accurately reflect the true nature and measurements of the structure.

In buildings that are very old or for which the blueprints are not available, a new set of drawings is needed. Someone with modest drafting abilities can produce usable drawings for the building. Careful measurement of the space will be transferred to a two-dimensional representation that serves as a basis for planning and design. An architectural firm can, of course, produce such drawings for a price. Often, usable drawings can be done by staff members even if structural details are lacking. It is usually wise to have accurate blueprints done by a reputable architect for any museum building, because structural problems and strengths will be identified that may have an impact upon future expansion and necessitate changes in either the building or its internal make-up.

Blueprints can be used as the basis for making more simplified drawings of galleries and exhibit spaces. In turn, these are employed to plan exhibitions.

By having the blueprints reproduced or by tracing them, a planner can make multiple copies of floorplans and elevations of the exhibit space.

The term floorplan refers to a drawing depicting the horizontal plane as viewed from directly above. Such plans include those characteristics and measurements critical to exhibit planning. Elevations are drawings that depict the vertical plane viewed straight on. They include salient characteristics and measurements. In a room consisting of four walls, one would generate four separate elevations.

A reflected ceiling plan is sometimes helpful when that part of a space is critical to the planning. When special constructions must abut the ceiling or there are to be special installations, this type of plan is useful. A reflected ceiling plan is a "floorplan" of the ceiling as seen lying on one's back looking straight up.

There are other drawings such as perspective renderings and isometric views. These may be produced as needed, but require a considerable understanding of architectural drafting. Usually, however, a floorplan and elevations will suffice for planning.

Models are a continuation of the drawing process, adding the dimension of depth. They may be quite simple as in figure 3.24, or much more complex and well-developed as in figure 3.25.

A chief advantage of using models is that a planner can get a practical sense of how the elements within an exhibit design will work. By moving around and over the model, the designer can examine all angles for problems and improvements that are invisible in a flat representation. Changes to a design are much simpler in a model than when they must occur while an exhibition is being installed, or worse, after the fact.

It is possible to work out colors, shapes, sizes, and spaces in detail using a scale model, thus saving much time and effort later. However, the very resources conserved by using the model are lost in creating it. Detailed models are time-consuming and require considerable effort and skill. This causes a dilemma: to model or not to model. In instances where time is short and the project is not especially complex, as a showing of paintings in a gallery, creating a model is probably not the wisest use of available resources. If, however, a new permanent gallery is being planned requiring many personnel-hours and much expense to accomplish, a scale model may be exactly the tool needed.

Another use of the model-making method is to work out, in advance, specific concerns involved with proper mounting and protection of delicate or rare objects to be exhibited. This may be more of a full-scale prototype construction than a small version, but the principal of exploring three-dimensional aspects of design is the same. Also, the use of models or prototypes for evaluative purposes is viable. A three-dimensional representation of a proposed design can provide a planner with the means to have others examine, try, touch, or activate an idea. By obtaining responses and opinions, the success of the idea can be assessed. This can be very helpful in developing interactive exhibits, and may avoid a common occurrence – the misuse or disuse of an exhibit element that was thought ideal in planning.

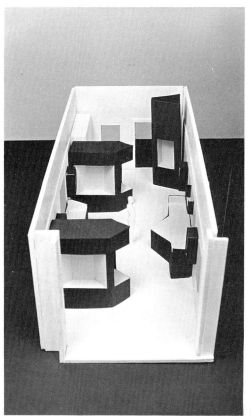

3.24 Simple model. A simple model contains little detail and often little color. It provides a means for conducting spatial experiments, establishing gallery layouts and plotting traffic patterns.

3.25 Complex model. A complex model employs color, surface detailing, material choices, labeling, even simulated artifacts to create a prototype of real space. Many design problems are solved using such models. They may include an entire gallery or only portions as seen here.

4

Controlling the exhibition environment

Any enclosed space – a box, room, or building – contains an environment. The environment is the total of the container's surroundings and circumstances. Any exhibition environment comprises two basic parts:

- matter (organic and inorganic materials)
- energy

As no matter/energy system is completely stable, the interaction of all the parts forms a constant state of action versus reaction. The conservation mission of a museum requires that such interactions be kept to a minimum. This means controlling the factors that promote interaction. In exhibitions, the environment of the presented objects needs to be understood as clearly as possible. The reason is a basic museological principle: the ethical and professional standard that collection objects must be cared for in a manner so as to preserve them for the foreseeable future. To provide adequate care for objects while on exhibit, environmental factors must be controlled as precisely as possible. The main factors to consider are:

- temperature
- relative humidity (RH)
- particulate matter and pollutants
- biological organisms
- reactivity of materials
- light

These are of primary concern in all collection management activities, of which exhibitions is one. In any system of matter and energy, the only achievable goal is to slow down the natural destruction of objects. By prioritizing collection management activities based upon the potential for harm, the process of decay can be slowed down dramatically.

Some of these exhibition concerns went unrecognized or ignored until a few years ago. New problems and solutions are becoming known as research in collection care is done. Staying abreast of the literature is more and more important for proper collection management – and more difficult.

external environment

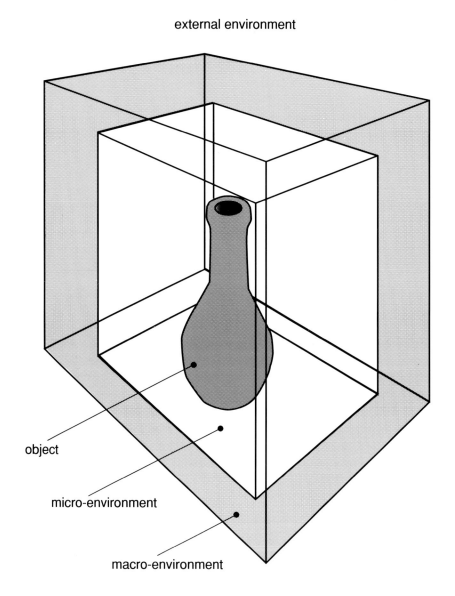

object

micro-environment

macro-environment

external environment

4.1 "Box-in-a-box" configuration of exhibition elements

Identification and scope

It is always preferable to identify potential problems and to take preventative measures. Recognition or identification often happens only after problems arise. Potential problems must be identified and their scopes determined in order to decide the most expedient method of control, whether proactive or reactive.

In some instances, it may be easiest to control the micro-environment rather than trying to control the whole building. A macro-environment may be defined as all the factors within a space that is room-size or larger, up to an entire building. A micro-environment is any smaller enclosure. Spaces such as display cases, vitrines, storage cabinets, or boxes are micro-environments.

Micro-environments are enclosed within and affected by the macro-environment outside them. Essentially, this configuration is described as a box-in-a-box.

Managing macro- and micro-environments addresses the same control factors. The principal difference is the size and scope of those factors.

Each exhibit case, vitrine, room, or box has its own internal climate. The tighter the box is sealed, the more self-contained the environment. If a display case is placed in a gallery, the macro-environment of the larger space influences the micro-environment of the smaller space.

Regulating the environment of the entire building is ideal. That way all parts are under the best of conditions. However, in many instances it may be best to control the micro-environments rather than trying to control the whole building, especially if the latter is not feasible.

Controlling macro- and micro-environments presents separate and distinct considerations. The main idea is to attempt to keep conditions in the environments as constant as possible. However, what is a sufficient control for a vitrine is not necessarily adequate for a building, or vice versa.

Macro-environments

To determine the control measures for a macro-environment, parameters must be established. To do that, it is necessary to have certain information available. The regional climate is especially important. Whether it is humid or dry, cold or hot, polluted or clean is all vital information. Temperature requirements for the collections need to be set. Is the optimum of 70°F (21°C) ± 2°, and 50% RH ±5% desirable or practical? If not, then what levels are acceptable and achievable? To what extent are airborne dust and pollutants a factor? What levels of these are permissible from a conservation standpoint? Setting the acceptable lighting, temperature, humidity, and environmental requirements comes first. In turn, those parameters drive the development of environmental control strategies.

The following are the major environmental factors for which control strategies are needed.

Temperature and relative humidity

A major part of exhibit designing involves modifying and enclosing spaces. Knowing the type and capabilities of the museum heating, ventilation, and air conditioning system (HVAC) is essential to the designer. Normally, local architects and air conditioning contractors are familiar with the HVAC needs of a particular region. They can suggest the proper equipment for museum needs.

HVAC systems are costly to purchase and install, must run continuously to maintain the desired macro-environment, and need constant monitoring and maintenance. Due to the expense of purchasing and installing HVAC systems, it is far more cost-effective to build them into new facilities, rather than retro-fitting them to an existing one. Many modern environmental control systems electronically monitor the facility climate continuously and effect changes as required.

In many museums, HVAC systems are not available or are too costly. In these institutions, climate control is more difficult, but not impossible. In areas of the world with high humidity, air conditioning systems are useful for removing moisture from the air as it enters the building. Passing incoming air over a cool surface causes water vapor to condense and collect in a trap, drying the air. Most HVAC systems employ either chlorofluorocarbons (CFCs) such as Freon, or chilled water for cooling. In addition to drying the air, HVAC systems also achieve the aim of cooling the air and removing some particulate matter.

Where HVAC systems for the entire museum are not feasible, room-size units may be substituted. These are cheaper to purchase, install, and operate. A refrigerated air conditioner can help maintain proper temperature levels in both exhibition and storage areas. Achieving temperature control means that relative humidity is more easily controllable.

If small air conditioning equipment is not available or practical, then using fans to circulate air, blocking windows that allow sunlight to enter, and insulating walls and ceilings can aid in reducing daily temperature fluctuations. The key is consistency. If a reasonably constant temperature can be maintained, then collections will remain more stable.

In areas where the relative humidity is normally low, the problem of re-humidifying the air is the concern. Injecting moisture back into the air after cooling it is the commonly used strategy. Humidifying can be done as a function of an air conditioning system or separately with a machine called a humidifier. When these devices are lacking, humidity management by sealing extremely sensitive materials in micro-environments with buffering agents may help.

One of the main activities in collection care is monitoring the environment. Control is not possible if the true conditions are not known. To monitor temperature and relative humidity in environments, some key tools are:

- thermohygrometers
- hygrothermographs
- psychrometers

What Is Relative Humidity?

At 0°F
(-17°C)
100% RH

At 70°F
(21°C)
6% RH

Humidity is the amount of water vapor in the air. Relative humidity (RH) is the amount of water vapor a given volume of air will hold *relative* to the amount it will hold at saturation at a certain temperature. As shown, a volume of air will hold more water vapor at a low temperature than it will hold at a warmer one. In an exhibit case, for example, this means that the higher the temperature, the lower the relative humidity.

4.2 Relative humidity

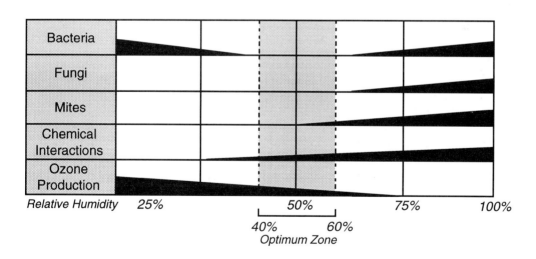

Bacteria
Fungi
Mites
Chemical Interactions
Ozone Production

Relative Humidity   25%   50%   75%   100%

40%   60%
Optimum Zone

4.3 RH ranges for potential collection threats

Methods of checking conditions in large spaces include the use of thermo-hygrometers and recording hygrothermographs. The "thermo-" portion of either word refers to temperature measurement. The "hygro-" portion denotes humidity. The suffix "meter" means a measurement indicator, and the ending "graph" signifies a record is kept. A hygrothermograph produces a paper record showing temperature and humidity levels over a fixed period. On the other hand, the thermohygrometer is read but does not produce a record.

There are many thermohygrometers on the market. It is wise to choose one that can be calibrated. Some devices are small enough to place within an exhibit case or vitrine and are unobtrusive. Recording hygrothermographs are larger due to the drive and recording mechanisms. Often these are placed on their own pedestal or mounted on the wall in an unobtrusive spot. Use of recording hygrothermographs to document conditions should be continuous. This allows the curator to stay familiar with the conditions to which the collection objects are subjected.

Placement of temperature and humidity monitoring equipment is critical. Locate them so they are in the same conditions as the objects. Thermo-hygrometers may be put inside the exhibit case or vitrine. Position larger instruments at the same height and under the same general conditions as the objects or cases. Placing an instrument close to the ceiling out of reach will produce unreliable results since temperature and humidity levels vary widely throughout a vertical gradient. The same is true of placing the monitoring equipment on the floor.

Psychrometers come in two basic forms. The sling psychrometer must be swung around to take a reading. Motor-driven or electronic types are also available. The psychrometer is needed for spot checks of conditions and to calibrate the hygrothermographs and thermohygrometers.

When thermohygrometers and the other sophisticated equipment are not available, then monitoring can still be done using thermometers and hygro-meters. Both of these are relatively inexpensive and are usually available.

Particulates and pollutants

Particulate matter (dust) and pollutants (airborne chemicals) pose another problem, usually solved by passing incoming air through a series of filters before it enters the building. In some cases, fiber filters are enough to remove dust and grit. In other cases, ionizing or other sophisticated filtering mechanisms are needed to remove very fine particles and airborne gases.

Household dust is a complex material. It is composed of many different compounds including plant and animal fibers, sand, industrial wastes, combustion by-products, and anything else that can be borne by air currents. Needless to say, many of these components are destructive to collections. The gritty sand particles are abrasive. Fibers provide food for pests. The chemical components can cause serious and irreversible damage to object surfaces.

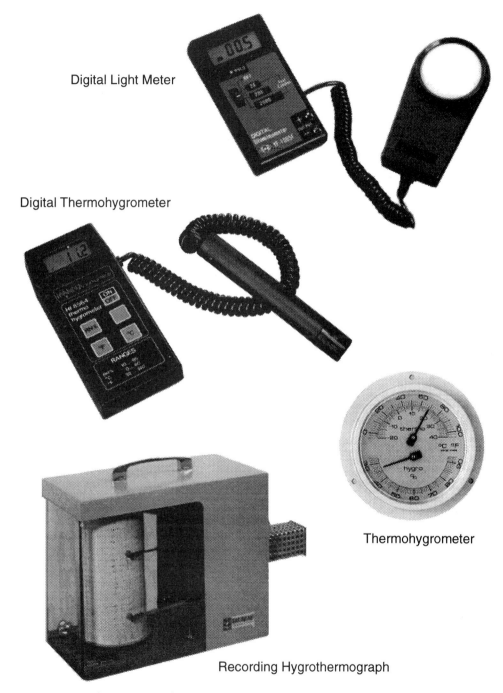

Digital Light Meter

Digital Thermohygrometer

Thermohygrometer

Recording Hygrothermograph

4.4 Environmental monitoring devices

Bamboo Powderpost Beetle
(Dinoderus minutus)

Powderpost Beetle
(Lyctus brunneus)

Common Carpet Beetle
(Anthrenus scrophulariae)

Larder Beetle
(Dermestes lardarius)

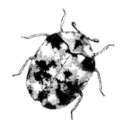

Furniture Carpet Beetle
(Anthrenus flavipes)

Webbing Clothes Moth
(Tineola bisselliella)

4.5   Museum insect pests

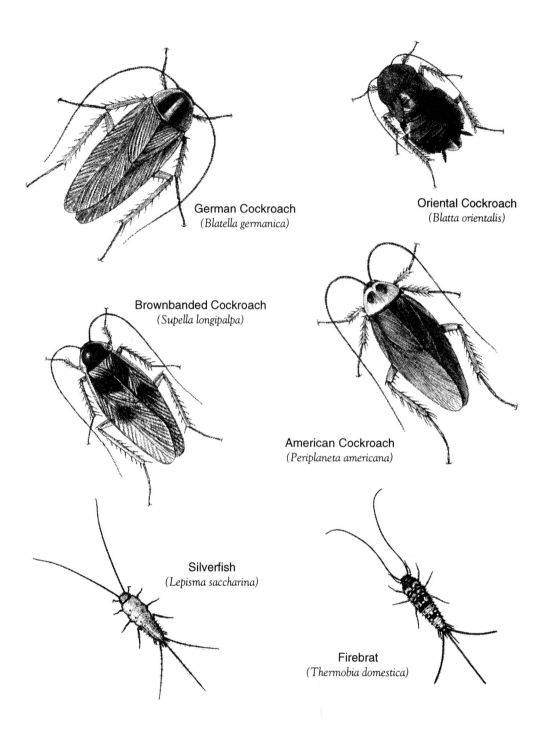

German Cockroach
(*Blatella germanica*)

Oriental Cockroach
(*Blatta orientalis*)

Brownbanded Cockroach
(*Supella longipalpa*)

American Cockroach
(*Periplaneta americana*)

Silverfish
(*Lepisma saccharina*)

Firebrat
(*Thermobia domestica*)

75

It is important to control the entry of dust into galleries and storage areas, but that is a very difficult task to accomplish, especially if the museum building is not sealed against the outside environment. Where possible, entry to exhibitions or even buildings should be through two sets of doors forming a dust trap between them. Housekeeping is critical in all circumstances. Cleaning and sweeping of the galleries should be done with materials that will attract and hold the dust. Damp mopping may assist in removing dust if no other options are available.

Airborne gases are a more difficult matter. Some HVAC systems are capable of filtering harmful gases. Most museums do not have such high-tech equipment. However, there are still actions that can be taken. Awareness is the first tool. Knowing what gases are present is essential. Knowing the effects of those vapors on collections is also essential. Highly susceptible materials may need to be sealed away from contact with outside air. Sometimes covering items can help. Open doors and windows should be closed to reduce the amount of fumes that enter the building. The use of air-locks (two-door entries) will reduce air exchange.

A fundamental rule of air pollution control is the prohibition of smoking in galleries, work areas, and collection storage rooms. Quite apart from the health considerations is the known damage to collections from exposure to tobacco smoke.

Control of organisms

The control of living organisms in exhibitions and collections is achieved through three main activities:

- monitoring
- prevention
- extermination

Insects, mammals, and microflora are the most common forms of collection pests.

Monitoring is the starting point for pest control. Sticky traps or light traps for insect pests should be a routine part of facility and collection management. These are inexpensive and easy to use. Identifying the kinds of organisms entering the museum can mean the difference between a pest outbreak and collection safety.

Collection inventories will discover infestations. However, inventory periods may be spaced a year apart. Spot checks of highly susceptible objects are needed on a more regular basis. Collection objects on exhibit are often more at risk than those in storage and should be checked once or twice a week for any signs of infestation.

Prevention is better than reaction. Proactive measures consist of reducing the opportunities and the resources necessary for living organisms to survive. Food in the form of crumbs, soft drink containers, gum and candy wrappers provide nourishment for invading pests. If a pest is sustained, it will lead to attacks on collections.

Careful examination of materials entering storage and exhibit areas for tag-along pests should be standard procedure. Food and drink should be prohibited from collection storage and exhibition areas. Regular facility cleaning along with perimeter extermination are preventative maintenance requirements.

If an infestation is detected, the type, extent, materials, and organisms involved, as well as the action taken, should be recorded in each object file (see the Infestation Report, Appendix 1). Conservators can recommend and accomplish the necessary actions first, to rid the affected area of pests, and second, to repair or contain the damage.

Reactivity of materials

Materials used in the construction of exhibitions pose their own set of potential collection care problems. Depending upon the museum building construction, the region where it exists, and the sources of the materials used to build it, a designer may need to consider buffering, ventilating, or sealing surfaces before placing objects on or around them.

If construction materials contain adhesives or corrosive substances, collection objects will need to be protected either by a barrier or by space. Since the possibilities are endless and unique to each situation, it is enough to say that the exhibit designer must be intimately acquainted with the facility, construction materials, and the requirements of the collections.

In the construction of exhibit furniture and mountings, it is even more important to be aware of the types of materials used. The objects are frequently enclosed inside exhibit cases and vitrines and exposed to whatever is sealed in with them.

Many substances produce chemicals and gases as a function of curing. The process of discharging vapors is called off-gassing. Woods produce several different acids and formaldehyde. Plywood, hardboard, and particle board release vapors from the adhesives used to bond them together. Many paints, finishes, and plastic products continually off-gas.

The construction materials in exhibitions are a very significant concern for designers. Oils, dust, and other chemicals released by building materials, and even the collection objects, have caused designers, curators, and conservators carefully to re-evaluate all installation practices for potential damage to collections.

Light

Another major environmental factor is energy. Energy is the necessary ingredient for all chemical and mechanical processes. Heat is a form of energy already discussed. Light, visible and invisible, is a major concern for all museum workers.

Natural sunlight contains all frequencies of electromagnetic energy or radiation. What we see is only a small portion of the whole spectrum and is not the most harmful form of radiation. It is the invisible that damages objects most.

Space Type	Design Level (FC)*
Auditoriums, classrooms	30
Conference rooms	30
Corridors, lobbies and means of access	15
Storage areas (general purpose)	10
Storage areas (need to examine details)	30
Service and public areas	15
Circulation areas	30

* A footcandle (FC) is a measure of illumination. 1FC = 10 lux.

In exhibit spaces, general illumination can often be kept well under 30 FC. Where conservation considerations are critical, the table below provides guidance in lighting objects to avoid UV damage.

Objects sensitive to UV	Maximum footcandles (FC)
Oil and tempera paintings, natural leather, horn, bone, ivory, lacquer	15 FC
Textiles, fabrics, tapestries, drawings, prints, watercolors, manuscripts, books, stamps, gouache, dyed leather, botanical specimens, skins, fur, feathers, insects	5 FC
Metal, stone, glass, ceramics, jewels, enamel and natural wood are not sensitive to UV radiation and maximum light levels need not be limited.	40 FC+*

* Some objects may be damaged by infrared (heat) and/or humidity to varying degrees. Levels should not exceed 40 FC as a rule.

4.6 Illumination levels

Radiation in the frequencies just below visible light is referred to as heat energy (infrared or IR). Heat has the effect of exciting or energizing the atoms and molecules within materials, making them more reactive and vulnerable.

Frequencies immediately above visible light are called ultraviolet (UV) light. This is a most harmful type of light for collections. High-energy ultraviolet rays have the effect of tiny bullets. They energize and damage the molecules within substances and promote chemical changes in the internal structure. In living organisms this causes sunburn and skin cancers. In non-living substances, it seriously degrades their molecular structures.

Some materials are extremely sensitive to ultraviolet. Materials like hair, feathers, leather, silks, ivories, and some dyes are particularly vulnerable to light damage. The literature concerning the effects of ultraviolet light on objects abounds, and more is being added as research continues.

Of the artificial light sources available for general illumination, fluorescent lighting produces the most ultraviolet rays. Incandescent lighting generates the most heat. Simple methods of limiting damaging radiation include ultraviolet filtering materials for fluorescent lights, and distance and ventilation for incandescent lighting.

Since light is necessary for the human eye to perceive objects, collections on exhibit are subjected to a certain degree of energy damage. The deterioration is cumulative and irreversible. However, proper management is the key to extending the exhibitable "life" of an object with only minor changes.

Adequate protection of collections must include a systematic approach to light management. Limiting exposure time and reducing light levels are the most effective means of preventing damage. Light meters that measure all frequencies of light, including visible and ultraviolet, are commercially available. A commonly used light meter is the kind used by photographers to measure visible light. Light levels are shown as either lumens or footcandles.

Using the minimum amount of light necessary to illuminate an object adequately is the management goal. Accomplishing this depends upon the amount of ambient light in the environment. Brightness and dimness are perceptions, not fixed levels of light. If a gallery is lit at three footcandles, then an object illuminated at five to ten footcandles will appear bright. In most cases, this level of light is acceptable for collections. Curatorial or conservation guidance is needed to determine the maximum light level for a given object. Exhibit lighting can be designed around such requirements in most situations. Devices such as fiber optics are now being used and developed that can provide light with virtually no ultraviolet or infrared components.

Special concerns of micro-environments

In many instances, an exhibit-maker will create small environments within larger ones. This configuration is known as a box-in-a-box (see Figure 4.1). It is in this configuration that the exhibit case or vitrine resides. The collection objects inside the cases and vitrines are exposed to small micro-climates.

The micro-environment represents a complex of variables. This environment is most critical since the collections are exposed directly to it. Temperature, relative humidity, material reactivity, and pest problems are all exaggerated in a smaller space.

A display case or vitrine is usually a sealed system except for the energy entering and leaving. In an exhibit case, lighting devices are internal and heat build-up is a major concern. In a vitrine, the external energy source may be several feet away but sufficient heat will still be trapped to affect the interior temperature significantly.

Higher energy levels present several problems. High temperatures increase molecular activity, heightening whatever chemical reactions are occurring. Remember, too, that relative humidity is directly related to temperature. The higher the temperature, the lower the relative humidity, causing desiccation.

Compounding the problem is the fact that lights will be switched on during public hours and off at night, creating rapid and sizable fluctuations in both temperature and relative humidity. These factors combine to create a potentially inhospitable climate for collection objects.

Methods of controlling micro-environments usually involve two approaches:

- Separating energy sources from the micro-environment as far as possible, thereby mitigating their impact.
- Placing buffering agents inside the micro-environment to reduce fluctuations.

Depending on the sensitivity of an object to light, heat, and humidity, one or both of these controls may be necessary. Materials like ivory, hair, feathers, woods, leather, silks, some stones, papers, and many dyes are markedly affected by environmental variations. Extra care must be taken to ensure stable conditions for these substances.

Since maintaining a stable energy level through continuous lighting is neither preferable nor cost-effective, energy levels will rise and fall. The most desirable method of buffering changes in humidity is one that automatically reacts to varying environmental conditions. There are two main methods of buffering environmental changes:

- Using the "natural" buffering effects of the objects and the construction materials.
- Using artificial buffering substances.

Many collection objects and building materials are "natural" buffers against environmental change. Wood, paper, latex paint, stone, cloth, and many other materials will react to changes in atmospheric heat and humidity by absorbing and releasing them. By placing collection objects in a micro-environment where the volume of air around the objects is roughly five times the volume of the objects, natural buffering will significantly assist in maintaining stable conditions.[1] On the other hand, a ratio of 50:1 will create an environment with no effective buffer.

It is the rapid fluctuations in heat and humidity that threaten the integrity of objects. Without buffers to slow and reduce the changes brought on by turning lights on and off, the atmospheric changes can be dramatic.

Several substances are hydrophilic (literally "water-loving") and have the inherent property of absorbing and releasing atmospheric water as conditions change. Silica gel is probably the most popular and best of the hydrophilic substances. This compound of silicon and oxygen reacts quickly to changes in atmospheric humidity. It is chemically inert and therefore very safe for objects. It can be bought "pre-set" to a specific relative humidity. Silica gel is available in granular form, in packets, or as compressed tiles. The placement of the gel can be designed into the exhibit case or vitrine so it is unobtrusive or invisible. The case needs to be tightly sealed or the silica gel will degrade and lose its buffering capabilities.

Some hydrated salts are also hydrophilic. The difficulties with these are that in some cases they are corrosive to objects, and they demand a high level of maintenance. Through constant melting and re-crystallizing, they can "creep" out of their containers and come in contact with collection objects. Although hydrated salts are not ideal, they do offer affordable solutions for relatively accurate humidity control.

Conclusions

The literature about conservation and curatorial issues in collection care is voluminous and ever growing. Designers ought to be as keenly aware of the concerns of collection maintenance as any other museum professional. Consultation with curators and conservators, as well as reading the literature, should be a priority matter for exhibit designers. Ignorance is not bliss when collection safety is at stake.

5

Exhibition administration

Exhibitions require a large degree of management and administrative effort, in addition to the collection and production activities. Museum administrators deal with many matters. These relate to the daily operations of the facility, personnel management, public relations, and financial and educational accountability. Among the administrative tasks are several that relate directly to exhibition planning and production. These are:

- scheduling and contracting for exhibitions
- contracting for services
- production and resource management
- documentation and registration
- publicity and marketing

Scheduling

Exhibitions are projects. They have definite beginnings and ends. Between are a certain number of activities that must take place to accomplish the project goal. That goal is the product – the exhibition itself. Exhibitions occupy space and require resources to produce, operate, and maintain.

There are two kinds of exhibition projects. They are defined on the basis of their duration:

- those of fixed length called temporary exhibitions
- those of indefinite length called permanent exhibitions

Typically, temporary exhibitions are on display for one year or less. However, "temporary" is subject to interpretation and can mean longer periods as well. Anything longer than three years is usually considered a long-term or "permanent" exhibition. Such rules are arbitrary and each institution may have its own definitions. It is important, however, that the definitions be clearly understood as they relate to the use of collection objects. Some objects are only suitable for short-term exposure to the exhibit environment – six months at best. The term "temporary" needs to reflect such constraints.

Assigning an exhibition to a specific time slot in the museum's list of activities is an activity called scheduling. Booking is the action of arranging with another museum or institution to borrow an exhibition.

The business of scheduling exhibitions is consigned to various persons within museum organizations. Who schedules really depends upon the staffing structure and job descriptions of the positions. In some cases, the registrar performs the role, but in others, an exhibitions or education staff member, or an administrator may have the duty. In a small museum, all scheduling and planning tasks may be the purview of one or two people. The main principle is coordination, regardless of the person or persons assigned.

Coordination and communication are essential. Every person involved in planning, managing, producing, and maintaining exhibitions must be aware of the project's progress. Note that people are fundamental to the success of any exhibition, and it is possible to accomplish only so many tasks with the time and personnel resources available. There are several matters to review when preparing to schedule exhibitions:

- available personnel
- available time
- accessible financial resources
- prior commitments
- other museum activities and projects
- national, religious, and local holidays
- community events such as special days, sporting events, commercial sales, market days, etc.
- the size of the galleries relative to the exhibition requirements

Staying abreast of these and other concerns is not easy. The exhibition scheduler should formulate a way of monitoring them. It helps to develop and use tracking documents such as that shown in Figure 5.1, and the Exhibition Request Form (Appendix 2).

The tracking process must begin and be centralized during the Conceptual Phase of exhibition development (see Chapter 1). For permanent exhibitions, the process of development is usually more prolonged. The important deadlines should be included in the exhibition scheduler's tracking document because they impact the ability of the staff to accomplish shorter-range tasks related to temporary exhibitions. Examining exhibition ideas, their relevance to the museum mission, and approving or rejecting them are responsibilities for the administration. Each exhibition on the approved list must be checked for both availability and feasibility. The necessary space, staff, and financial resources are identified. If the essential resources are at hand, the exhibition is scheduled, and planning and development can begin.

DATES		Gallery 1	Gallery 2	Gallery 3	Gallery 4
Jul	5	(Apr 14, 1991)	(Nov 17, 1991)	(Mar 1, 1992)	(Jun 8, 1992)
	12				
	19		Diamond		
	26	Diamond	M:		
Aug	2	M:	People		Through the
	9	Sculptures		Sculptures	Viewfinder:
	16			from the	Photography
	23		change	Collection	from the
	30		exhibits		Collection
Sep	6				
	13	Sep 13			
	20		Diamond M:		
	27		Selections:		
Oct	4	Sep 24	Trees. etc.		
	11	John			
	18	Pavlicek			
	25	Exhibition			
Nov	1	Nov 1			
	8				
	15			Nov 1	
	22	Nov 15			
	29			Romare	Nov 29
Dec	6	Robert		Bearden	
	13	Henri		Prints	
	20	& Lacquer			
	27	Boxes			
1993	3	Jan 3		Jan 3	
Jan	10				Jan 10
	17			Jan 17	
	24	Jan 24			
	31				
Feb	7	Souvenirs		Art of	Face, Faced,
	14			Private	Facing
	21			Devotion	

5.1 Gallery schedule

Contracting

There are several situations in exhibition development that require working with contractual agreements. Temporary exhibitions include those produced in-house by a museum using its own and borrowed collection items. They also include circulated traveling exhibitions from institutions and commercial exhibition services.

Whether borrowing the whole exhibition or a few collection items for exhibiting, the transactions will usually involve a legal contract. If not a "contract" *per se*, they will at least have a letter of agreement stipulating conditions and expectations. Contracts for traveling exhibitions usually contain at least the following elements:

- the official title of the exhibition
- the dates of the loan
- the exhibition rental fee
- a fee payment schedule
- cancellation provisions
- publicity stipulations and restrictions
- insurance requirements
- transportation requirements, costs, and arrangements
- security requirements
- other provisions specific to the particular transaction such as catalog availability and sales, special requirements for the ones who install, lecturers, or demonstrators that accompany the exhibition, etc.
- signature blocks for the representatives of the agreeing institutions

Traveling exhibition services and reputable museums are normally very careful to make contractual agreements straightforward, without hidden pitfalls. Unfortunately, some exhibition sources may not be so ethical. It is always wise to have contracts reviewed by a person who is familiar with such arrangements. Items to beware of are:

- hidden shipping costs
- excessive requirements for security, insurance, publicity, packing, etc.
- hidden agreements to pay travel and housing costs for consultants, the ones who install, lecturers, etc.
- highly inflated insurance valuations
- severe or unrealistic cancellation penalties
- unreasonable liability stipulations
- items that put the museum under unusual obligation for fees, handling, security, publicity, or other matters

Another area of contractual agreement concerns collection loans. The methods and standards of loaning objects should be clearly delineated in the loan policies and procedures of both the borrowing and lending institutions. The provisions of the loan, its duration, the method of review, return, and renewal are set out in writing. The loan document clearly defines the roles and expectations of both institutions. A loan agreement should include the following information as a minimum:

- a description of the loan object
- accession number
- catalog number
- purpose of the loan
- duration of the loan

- insurance requirements
- publicity restrictions and credit lines
- transportation provisions
- review periods
- special conditions of the loan
- places for agent signatures of the agreeing institutions

A further form of contract is that dealing with services and products. In some instances, exhibitions are contracted, in part or in total, to agencies outside the museum. In such cases, legally binding contracts are written and signed. Again, it is wise to have such contractual obligations reviewed by a person or persons familiar with these matters.

When dealing with contractors, the museum should always maintain right of approval for all plans and fabrication. It is important to establish the client–supplier relationship at the beginning of a project and to have clearly instituted lines of communication, review, and approval. At the start of the project, the contractor and museum's representative should outline the whole project and the desired outcome. They should establish deadlines and progress reporting methods – in short, a timeline.

Production and resource management

As mentioned in Chapter 1 on exhibition development, essential management activities deal with the availability of resources. The elements required to accomplish any task are time, money, and people. This translates into five management activities:

- time management
- money management
- quality control
- communication
- organizational control

To assess and track these activities effectively takes administrative tools. Different organizations and administrators have their own particular apparatuses for managing resources. However, at least two documents are needed: a checklist of activities and a timeline.

Checklists

The management tool that incorporates all stages of the process is the exhibit checklist (see the Checklist for Exhibition Development, Appendix 3). The checklist includes budgetary information, task assignments, a timeline, and other essential developmental elements. It serves as a tracking document for the scheduler and project manager that is specific to the exhibition. It is a quick reference to the exhibition's current stage of development.

Although the checklist may be tailored to fit any museum's exhibition development process, it needs to include a few basic elements. These are:

- a method of determining a project's status
- a budgeting section both for obtaining funds and for their dispersal
- a timeline of required tasks
- task assignments

The checklist should reflect the initiation and evaluation activities used in making the decision to go forward with an exhibition. Determining status may consist of a list of steps through which an exhibition idea must pass before being approved for scheduling. It can also include other procedural landmarks that show the exhibition's current stage of development. A series of checkmarks and dates makes it easy to find out how far the processes of planning, production, and fabrication have progressed.

Timelines

To accomplish any task, a sequence of activities and events must take place to realize the product. A timeline, or series of deadlines, is needed. The exhibit timeline is the management tool for sequencing (see the Checklist for Exhibition Development, Appendix 3). It details the tasks and needs leading to a pre-established opening date for the exhibition, and ensures that all parties are apprized of developments and needs. Through deadlines it motivates timely availability of essential elements.

Setting up a timeline begins with assigning an opening date (the project goal) for the exhibition. Everything on the timeline is then related to the opening. The timeline should show all pertinent actions (the project objectives) in the planning and production of the exhibition from initiation to termination.

A timeline is also a tool for evaluating the practicality of the development process. There are always ways to improve any procedural activity. By evaluating whether deadlines were met for a given exhibition, future projects can be planned more effectively.

Documentation

Every collection activity requires the careful keeping of records. This provides a reliable history for the collection objects upon which future assessments and conservation efforts may be founded. Documentation should be generated and kept in two main forms: whole exhibition information (exhibition file) and individual object data (object file). Normally, these types of information are not kept together. The information generated about an exhibition is usually placed in the administrative or exhibition offices. Materials related to the collection objects are stored in the collection and registration files.

Collection files should reflect any loans of objects for exhibition purposes and the accompanying condition reports. Conservation measures, special preparations, or other treatments of collection objects must be recorded and placed in the object files.

To keep all the information about an exhibition together and to be able to track progress, the scheduler must maintain or have access to the exhibition file. Each exhibition should have a folder that contains all pertinent materials. This includes exhibition ideas, schedules, contracts, timelines, checklists, object lists, storylines, catalogs, and other similar information. These files should be permanently retained. Indeed, it is a good idea to keep duplicate records off-site. The exhibition files form a repository of the museum's exhibition history and serve as a reference for evaluation and possible inquiries.

Publicity and marketing

The nature of most societies today, especially in developed countries, demands the use of publicity and marketing to attract the population's attention to leisure activities. There are many forms that publicizing and advertising of exhibitions can take. To know what strategies to employ, the audiences must be identified. It is helpful to employ a marketing specialist to assist with these matters, but most institutions cannot afford to do so. Instead, staffs must assess audiences, their needs and expectations, and then generate methods of informing the public of the museum's offerings.

Methods often used to communicate what the museum is doing are brochures, pamphlets, mailers or fliers, newsletters, posters, announcements of openings or acquisitions, and catalogs. However, these forms of public advertisement generally reach only the museum's current audiences. In more recent years, commercial advertisement and marketing techniques have been applied to museum exhibitions and programs. Printed and electronic media have been used to promote interest and attract audiences. The blockbuster exhibitions such as "King Tut" and "Ramses" used all forms of media and marketing skills to sell the exhibitions. In dollars and cents, they were highly effective. In the area of heightening and changing the public awareness and perceptions of museums, they have been dynamic.

For most museums, however, marketing is a matter for the museum staff. Few budgets allow for the hiring of consultants, or provide large sums for publicity. Yet, even within such constraints, there are actions that can provide a positive and visible presence for the museum in its community.

Coordinating museum activities with community events and interests can gain a museum much free publicity from the local media. Activities that relate to seasonal celebrations can also relate to museum collections and educational goals. For instance, flying kites is a seasonal activity in many parts of the world. By promoting and sponsoring a Kite Day on the museum grounds, many visitors can be attracted that otherwise would not approach the museum.

Such events have the effect of making the museum a place for families and friends to gather, thus promoting a sense of comfortableness. Art fairs, demonstrations, astronomy viewing nights, holiday celebrations, open-house events – all can promote a feeling of belonging for a community and its museum.

Administering all these activities, in addition to the printed and electronic outreach efforts, involves much effort. Again, the critical elements of time, personnel, and money need to be coordinated. Publicity and marketing plans should be part of the planning process for an exhibition just as surely as the gallery plan. Ideally, a person should be specifically assigned to preparing and executing publicity and marketing activities for the museum. However, many museums simply can not afford such a position. Also, hiring a professional firm to oversee promotional duties is feasible only occasionally.

Many exhibitions do not need exceptional publicity efforts. However, capitalizing on an exhibition that has the potential for creating a great deal of interest and attracting new audiences is wise. Such opportunities may occur only once or twice a year, or less. It is very important to make the most of these "local blockbusters."

The museum staff can accomplish many of the publicity needs for their institution without hiring consultants or new staff. Contacting the local media, preparing and distributing press packets, and inviting media personalities to participate in public activities can help promote the museum's interests. A press packet might include a one-page statement about the exhibition, a schedule for the exhibition and concurrent activities, and representative photographs of objects from the exhibition. Also, it is a good idea to include in the packet a brochure or handout about the museum, public hours, admission fees, and like information. The museum should prepare press kits containing generic museum information in advance, and then when promoting an exhibition is contemplated, the specific exhibition information can be added. This way kits can be assembled quickly and distributed when publicity for an exhibition opening is desirable.

In many places, news broadcasts are presented during the late afternoon or evening. Mentioning an exhibition during these programs is likely to gain much public attention. Often people make leisure-time decisions spontaneously as a response to their most recent stimulus. The immediacy of the broadcast media makes them good tools to get the museum's message out to the public.

In the United States, the rules governing the broadcast media require that stations present a certain number of free, public-service hours of programming. Public-service announcements (PSAs) present an opportunity for publicity on which museums should capitalize. Working with local television and radio stations to prepare PSAs is a cost-effective method of producing professional advertising. The main disadvantage of PSAs is that they are seldom aired during the peak viewing or listening hours. These hours of "prime time" are too commercially valuable to the stations. However, a good working relationship with the local media can encourage station management to present the museum's messages at acceptable times during the broadcast day.

Employing creative thinking and promoting good relations with local media can help a museum meet many of its own publicity needs. As museums continue to compete for public attention and attendance, publicity and promotion will be increasingly important.

6

Exhibition evaluation

The area of museum exhibition evaluation is one that has gained some prominence in the past decade. There is now a sizable amount of information in the literature about the why and how of evaluation. It is not the intent of this chapter to attempt to cover all of the information now available on exhibition evaluation. Rather, it is intended as an overview or introduction to the rationale and use of evaluation as it relates to museum exhibitions in general.

To evaluate is to rate or measure something. To evaluate exhibitions is to question their effectiveness and to learn from their successes and failures. Learning and growing involve a continual process of evaluating, and consciously or not, every exhibit planner is involved in evaluating the products. Yet, deliberate evaluation is often neglected in exhibition planning. In fact, many museums make no provision for gathering evidence as to whether their exhibition efforts are successful or not. Whether they accomplish their goals is an unknown quantity, subject to supposition rather than supportable evidence. For some organizations, lack of interest may be a factor. For others, ignorance or willful denial are causative agents.

Some exhibit developers have the attitude that exhibition content, design, planning, and presentation are the exclusive domain of museum professionals, not to be diluted or corrupted by outside input or undue scrutiny. In the past that attitude has fostered a sort of benign dictatorship over the public exhibitions in museums. Exhibitions created against such a backdrop are characterized by the idea that professional, in-house curators, designers, and administrators somehow know what is suitable and appropriate for the public without the benefit of feedback from the intended audience.

In the last two or three decades, museums have been classified as "leisure-time activities," while still retaining an identity as intellectual centers. Museums now compete for a share of the public attention with non-intellectual establishments like shopping malls, cinemas, sporting events, and other such popular institutions and activities. Educational pursuits are not always viewed as enjoyable or desirable by the leisure-seeking populace. To offset the somewhat stilted reputation that museums possess in the public mind, they have had to look to self-studies and marketing strategies to help identify ways to make their products more palatable and attractive. It has become clear that serving the needs and desires of the public is necessary for maintaining a viable position in modern society. Improving the appeal of the museum experience without sacrificing its intellectual integrity has replaced an elitist, academic attitude for many institutions. While presenting problems of maintaining institutional standards when carried too far, this need for leisure-time allure has its positive side. Competition has forced the museum community to seriously reassess the relevance of what it believes and does in relation to a modern world.

What to evaluate

In the effort to determine the best means of addressing this new externalized, competitive mission, museums have searched for a foundation upon which to base planning and decisions. Many have fallen into a trap of depending upon attendance figures as the indicator of how well exhibitions are succeeding.

On the surface, attendance appears ideal for judging success or failure, and it is easy to determine. This has led, in some instances, to the popularization, glamorization, and promotion of public exhibitions to generate visitor numbers without due consideration for educational content or meaning. However, as with most things easily gained, mere numbers say very little about success in the areas where museums are truly able to excel. Attendance figures can never reveal the effectiveness of communication. While it can be argued credibly that if a person walks through an exhibition, he or she has in some degree been affected by the experience, whether or not there is such a perception by the individual, exhibition effectiveness must be judged in relation to how well it provides perceptible learning experiences.

> "It is important to keep in mind just who is visiting an exhibit and what kinds of expectations these individuals may have."[1]

The effectiveness of exhibitions in meeting expectations and providing educational value is more difficult to rate than visitor counts. Comprehensive, concrete ways to measure the interaction between exhibits and people are required. To do this, it is necessary to ascertain what the parameters are. As with any analysis, one must set down the framework of the problem, identify the elements, and formulate a series of questions to be answered.

> In evaluating an exhibit, some questions to ask might include:
>
> ● Does the exhibit attract and hold visitor attention, and if so, how well and for how long?
> ● Are visitors learning anything?
> ● Does the exhibit meet the needs of people? Does the exhibit address and answer their questions?
> ● Do visitors feel the museum experience is personally rewarding?
> ● Does the exhibit stimulate continuing interest in the subject?
> ● Will the visitors return to the museum, and why or why not?

Visitor numbers do not indicate whether anyone is taking away knowledge. As with commercial concerns, "sales" figures are needed to get a firm grasp on how well museums are doing educationally. Like the merchant, the exhibition planner must listen to the customer complaints as well as praises. The shelves of knowledge must be carefully packaged and then observed to see what sells and what is left untouched. Assessing the level of knowledge possessed by the visitor before, during, and after his or her visit is a reasonable way of determining exhibition success or failure. If the level of a patron's understanding or appreciation before he or she enters the exhibition can be compared to the level upon leaving, a valuable piece of information can be established: whether or not the exhibition communicates. If it does, then education is happening. Following that discovery, the next question will involve how efficiently it communicates. There is always room for improvement.

> In planning to evaluate, certain parameters must be determined. These include:
>
> ● What are the data required to do an evaluation?
> ● How are the data to be collected?
> ● Is evaluation to be scientific or perceptual, objective or subjective, formal or informal, cognitive or affective?
> ● What is to be evaluated?

How to answer the question of effective communication is often confusing to the novice evaluator. Terms such as front-end analysis, formative and summative testing, and naturalistic or goal-referenced evaluation are used in the literature. The terminology can be daunting, but no matter the vocabulary, the real challenge is to determine whether and how well the exhibition is accomplishing its purpose of communicating. The exhibition purpose and intent are conscious determinations made by the museum staff. It is those expressed as goals and objectives that provide the basis for evaluating exhibition effectiveness. When speaking of evaluation, one will always end up talking about goals and objectives.

> ". . . evaluation is the process used to test and determine
> whether the goals (and specific exhibit features) are
> working out as planned."[2]

Evaluation goals might include:

● Is the museum cognizant of and knowledgeable about its audiences?
● Does the museum have effective mechanisms for gaining input from the community?
● What are the served community expectations and needs?
● Does the museum have a well-defined process for gathering and sifting ideas for exhibitions?
● Are there ways to improve the planning and production of exhibitions?
● When visitors go through an exhibition, do they gain knowledge, understanding, or appreciation?
● Do visitors repeatedly return to the museum? Why or why not?

As a first step a museum staff needs to write down what the evaluation is to achieve. Three targets areas for exhibition evaluation are:

● museum audience
● exhibition process
● exhibition effectiveness

The need and criteria for evaluation should have been established and written down before beginning the Planning Stage of the Developmental Phase (see Chapter 1). If they are not, then much of the early effort of evaluating may be spent reconstructing goals and objectives. Even if they are not in written form, the implied goals can usually be deduced from the exhibition and the planning process. No matter how goals and objectives are originally expressed, to be useful they must be quantifiable and measurable.

Before goals and objectives for the exhibition can be set down, it is necessary to know the audience well. The real goal for audience evaluation is to determine if the visitor is responding to the exhibition by learning and feels the experience meets his or her expectations. There are many sources of information concerning the museum audience ranging from a personal knowledge of the community by living in it to formal studies such as demographic and psychographic surveys often conducted by city governments or commercial interests to determine constituent needs and expectations.

Information that can be valuable to museum exhibit-planners might include determining:

- What visitors expect from exhibitions and the museum.
- Ways to improve visitor orientation.
- Which words communicate most effectively.
- Visitor conceptual orientation.
- Visitor traffic patterns and problems.
- Whether interpretive elements work as planned.
- Whether labels are being read and if they are communicating.
- If audiovisual and hands-on features work and are durable.

From the assessment of the exhibition planning and presentation process, the museum gains new and more intimate knowledge of its own inner workings, and its strengths and weaknesses. By carefully examining and applying knowledge about how things get done in an organization, improvements can almost certainly be made. Everything should be considered from initiation of ideas for exhibitions, through the selection and scheduling phases, up to and including dismantling the exhibition and planning for the next one. This creates an information loop back into planning for future exhibitions. This continuing, cyclical process should be evolutionary, not stationary in nature.

The effectiveness of the exhibition as an educational, inspirational presentation can only be measured by testing the impact it has on an audience. There must be carefully described outcomes set down before the exhibition project begins that can then be tested to ascertain whether or not goals are being met.

C. G. Screven, a noted researcher in the field of evaluation, raises three essential questions about goals and evaluation:[3]

(1) "What impact should the exhibit have on visitors (or what impact do you want)?"

The answer to this question must be within the context of the stated goals and objectives for the exhibition. "Good exhibit evaluation must begin with clarification of goals for an exhibit in terms that relate objects, interpretation features, and the physical design of space to visitors."[4] It should be pre-determined in the planning of an exhibition, either by implication or specific statement, exactly what the exhibition is to accomplish, how the visitors are supposed to interact with the exhibition, what information they should gain, and what changes in attitude or appreciation are desired.

(2) "How will the desired goals be achieved (or how will you attempt to achieve this impact via your exhibit)?"

The museum must specifically state what is expected of the exhibition (goals) and then how those goals are to be met (objectives). The task is to determine how objectives can be targeted to visitor needs and desires, and then quantified so that the results are measurable.

(3) "How can it be known whether the exhibit goals and objectives have the desired impact on the intended audience?"

The evaluators must have a good understanding of the knowledge or emotional base of the visitors. This can only be obtained by pre-visit assessments such as interviews, questionnaires, or surveys. Having established the level of understanding in advance, the audience may then be tested after viewing the exhibition to determine whether it has had the desired impact on knowledge and attitudes. Post-visit interviews, questionnaires, and surveys can garner raw information. Comparing actual learning gained or attitudes affected with the established goals and objectives will give a sense of how successfully the exhibition has communicated.

When to evaluate

Testing is the process of gathering data and using them to compare goals and objectives against results. Pre-testing, or front-end analysis, is not so much concerned with effectiveness of the exhibition as with building the foundation for setting goals and objectives.

Evaluating exhibitions for their effectiveness can occur within two primary timeframes: (1) during the planning and production of the exhibition, and (2) after the exhibition is complete and open to the public. Evaluation during the first period is called formative evaluation, and during the latter, summative. By formulating tests to measure the relationship between what the exhibition planners intended and what actually happened, the effectiveness of the planning and design can be checked.

In formative evaluation, testing occurs during the exhibition's development while changes can still be made. In-progress testing may be done as many times as needed or as deemed effective. Early front-end analysis by way of questionnaires and interviews of potential audience segments can help establish target audiences and pre-visit educational levels. Formative evaluation provides direct input for exhibition planners and designers about what does or does not work. Pre-tests can include a number of different data collection activities:

- audience surveys
- pre-visit analyses of visitor knowledge and attitudes

- marketing research
- demographic and psychographic analyses
- feasibility studies

Trying out design elements and interpretive ideas often takes the form of mock-ups, models, or mini-exhibits. These pre-production prototypes can reveal much about the effectiveness of a design, as well as providing valuable information about other elements such as content, material durability, communication effectiveness, conservation standards, and any number of other concerns. Specific design applications and presentation formats can be tested very economically early on, thereby avoiding expensive failures or changes later. What seems simple to the designer is not always so obvious to the visitor. There is no way to intuitively know whether a design or communication format will work. Only testing and experience can provide for an educated guess.

A simple formative test might involve an interactive device, such as a flip-cover question and answer panel, built of inexpensive materials like mat board. The panel can be placed in a lobby, hallway, gallery, or other public area inviting visitors to participate. By observing and questioning people who try the device, the staff can get a good sense of how successful a similar idea would be in an exhibition environment. Also, if the presented information reflects the level and type intended for the final exhibition, then the degree of successful communication can be checked. Regardless of the expertise of any designer or planner, no one can know what will or will not communicate unless their ideas have been tested.

Not only methods, but also materials can be tested for durability and usability. In one instance, a particular plastic product was placed on the floor where the staff would walk on it for some weeks. The results of this test helped the designers determine that the substance could withstand the handling it would be subjected to in actual use by school children. Any such testing of materials or methods is a kind of formative evaluation.

Summative evaluation, on the other hand, assesses the product after it is completed. Such tests are useful for identifying problems and improving effectiveness of exhibitions. Summative evaluation also provides vital data for planning future exhibitions.

Follow-up evaluation might involve pre- and post-visit interviews to determine the level of information being transferred through the exhibition, mapping and timing of visitor activity in the gallery, or the use of questionnaires to assess satisfaction with the exhibition. Based upon the educational goals already established, the interview process can reveal how well those goals are being met. In some instances, such as for permanent galleries, adjustments and changes to the exhibition are still possible. Regardless of whether the current exhibition can practicably be altered, the information gained through summative testing will be invaluable for future planning.

Summative testing is administered as a post-installation activity, usually based on visitor interviews or questionnaires. Often these assessments are one-time activities and are performed to determine how the exhibition is perceived and used by the public. Such evaluations assist future exhibition planning by describing visitor needs, assessing actual audience composition, generating ideas for better interpretation, and aiding in establishing more realistic exhibition goals.

> **"In fact, the purpose of exhibition evaluation is to find out how visitors are reacting to objects and exhibition features and thereby determine whether an exhibition is working the way it was planned."**[5]

The whole idea behind evaluation is the improvement of exhibition execution and performance. Testing the audience before and after viewing the exhibition will provide information about its communicative viability. Observing changes and wear in materials will provide knowledge about where and when to use them. Assessing the frequency and duration of use by visitors will supply information about what does or does not attract attention as planned.

Front-end analyses and formative and summative evaluations are complementary, not exclusionary. Pre-testing is useful in determining who the audience are and what they expect. Formative evaluation assists in planning, and summative assessments tell whether that planning was successful. By conducting testing in all three timeframes, a more complete picture of the exhibition development process, the goals and objectives, targeted audiences, and the effectiveness of communication can be drawn.

How to evaluate

There are any number of approaches to evaluating or testing. Each researcher has his or her own particular methodology and procedure. In many cases, a newcomer to exhibition evaluation is daunted by the confusing claims of the various potential approaches. Really, there are only a few ways to go about evaluation with many variations. A principal manner of identifying data collection methodologies is to classify them as either formal (scientific, quantitative data gathering procedures and interpretation aimed at determining precise levels of learning and retention), or informal (perceptual, less structured, aimed at determining reactions and usefulness).

Formal methods are characterized by clearly defining goals and objectives and quantifiable, testable components. To obtain quantifiable goals, the evaluating and planning become integrated. This is called a "goal-referenced approach."[6]

According to C. G. Screven, there are two main properties of this approach:

(1) Distinct decision points at which it is determined how well goals and visitor reaction match.

(2) Feedback from evaluation of exhibition components to accomplish desired outcomes.

Goal-referenced evaluation can be done for existing or future exhibitions. In either case, Screven indicates three tasks ought to be incorporated:

(1) Define the intended audience.

(2) Define the visitor-related goals (including educational goals and objectives).

(3) Develop dependable measures of visitor reactions, such as knowledge or attitudes, to determine whether goals are being met.

Another, more informal approach to evaluation relies upon neither firm exhibition nor evaluative goals. This is called exploratory evaluation, sometimes referred to as the perceptual method. This type of testing yields descriptive information that can be used in exhibition planning. R. G. Barker's methods emphasize the importance of the physical setting to evaluative behavior (relating the physical conditions and the expectations of the visitors).[7] This method introduces a number of affective factors including a visitor's perception of the museum/gallery, his or her worldview, and behavioral/cultural norms. The perceptual method treats the exhibition and the visitor as a single unit or at least as co-dependents.

Robert Wolf, another evaluation expert, uses what he calls "naturalistic evaluation."[8] This too is related to setting and behavior. Wolf emphasizes unobtrusive observations and conversational-style, post-visit interviews. He advocates a less structured format, not inhibited by pre-stated objectives. This, Wolf maintains, allows for unexpected and enlightening revelations.

These informal evaluation methods have commonalaties. Wolf and Tymitz describe three steps in the strategy of the naturalistic evaluation.[9] They are in essence:

- Assess the characteristics of the whole exhibition setting. Exhibitions do not occur in a vacuum. It is important to understand the whole context of the museum experience.
- Identify the elements in an exhibition that appear to have the greatest influence on the visitor.
- Select those elements that appear most important in controlling what happens in the exhibition. That is, narrow the list of parts identified in the second step to those that should be studied in depth.

Wolf outlines six sources of data or information used to determine the above:

- General descriptive information about the physical and institutional setting.
- Action or behavior descriptions from observing visitors in the museum and exhibition setting.
- Quotable quotes from the visitors that reflect their impressions about the exhibition experience.

- Physical traces of past behavior such as places worn smooth by rubbing, points on maps that have been obliterated from much touching, and other such signs of visitor impact on the exhibits.
- Written records.
- Interviews with staff, professionals, and visitors to gather salient concerns to consider.

Informal evaluations, though not scientific, can yield valuable information for the exhibiting institution and may be summative or formative, cognitive or affective. Cognitive evaluation seeks to determine what concrete information a visitor has gained from the exhibition, while affective evaluation assesses changes in attitude or appreciation about the subjects presented in the exhibition.

Formal evaluation methods are more useful for gathering cognitive information. Cognitive testing can involve pre- and post-visit interviews to determine what visitors know, or think they know, about a subject before they experience the exhibition. Afterwards they are tested to see if factual information has been learned. Much of cognitive testing depends on interviews or questionnaires. The information gained can be quantified and set down in readily digestible reports showing learning curves and other useful data that will support the assessment of the exhibition's successes or failures.

Affective evaluation is more difficult to obtain because it deals with intangibles – attitudes and beliefs. These are less easily quantified into numerical values. Since affective learning is more abstract, it is more difficult to discover why and how it occurs. From evaluations of affective learning, the best one can get is a sense of success or failure.

Unobtrusive observation – noting where visitors linger to look or read, noticeably react to or discuss the subject matter, or smile and show pleasure with the exhibition – leads to a sense of positive outcome. However, if the visitors avoid certain exhibitions, leave quickly, show displeasure, or speak negatively, the reasons are not so easily discovered. Assessing what is not working and why requires going beyond simple success or failure judgments. Questions must be asked of the visitors in ways that are designed to elicit honest appraisal and emotional responses.

Scientific and perceptual approaches both need adequate input to be useful. There are a number of effective ways to gather data for more in-depth analysis, such as:

- formal interviews
- open-ended discussions
- written questionnaires
- cognitive and/or affective tests
- unobtrusive observation, involving:
    tracking and timing visitors as they move through various exhibitions
    observational checklists and behavioral rating sheets to codify visitor behavior
    videotape and analysis

To obtain data as free of bias as possible, certain precautions must be built into the testing. Sampling must include a large enough segment of the museum visitor population to provide reliable results. It must be random as to who is observed or questioned, and the time of day, week, and year should be varied to avoid pattern and bias creeping into the data. These are standard sampling procedures and are covered much more thoroughly in other sources.

Conclusions

What kinds of information can evaluation provide for museums? In reality, the list is endless and depends solely upon the goals of the evaluator and the design of the tests. However, museums can learn much from within the parameters established in existing questionnaires and interview techniques.

More important than determining the effectiveness of design elements is ascertaining whether the visitor is learning anything and whether he or she feels the experience is worth their time.

Marilyn Hood's six criteria for choosing leisure-time activities.[10]

- being with other people
- doing something worthwhile
- feeling comfortable and at ease
- challenging new experiences
- having the opportunity to learn
- participating actively

To make value judgments about the effectiveness of the exhibition, criteria for filtering and distilling the data must be in place. How can it be established whether the exhibition was successful or not? There is no clear set of criteria upon which all agree. The criteria suggested by museum professionals such as designers, educators, and curators are not altogether those of the visitors, as revealed in a survey done by M. B. Alt and K. M. Shaw at the Natural History Museum, London.[11] Visitors were asked to define what they considered to be the characteristics of an ideal exhibition. Among the findings were the following criteria:

- It (the exhibition) makes the subject come to life.
- It gets the message across quickly.
- You can understand the point(s) it is making quickly.
- There is something in the exhibition for all ages.
- You can't help noticing the exhibition.

Museum professionals were also asked about their criteria for a successful exhibition. Although the list is longer, and as might be expected more detailed and directed to staff needs, many similarities are to be found. Attractiveness, ease of comprehension, and the ability to hold audience attention are common traits. All of these aspects lead to one overriding criterion for the success of an exhibition: that is, the exhibition must communicate well. Attention, attractiveness, and all other considerations must work together to accomplish that end.

The criteria as expressed by museum professionals were more formal and less indicative of public attitudes:[12]

- Is the exhibition attractive to visitors?
- Is the exhibition easily comprehended by visitors?
- Will visitors perceive the exhibition as a unified concept or setting? Is there a focus?
- Do exhibition components attract attention?
- Do exhibition components hold attention?
- Is the exhibition presentation viewed as appropriate for the content involved?
- Do visitors think exhibition information presented is accurate?
- How well does the exhibition handle crowd flow?
- Does the exhibition match visitor characteristics?
- How well do (interpretive) materials work?
- How do visitors perceive the exhibition relating to surrounding areas or other exhibitions?
- How do visitors evaluate the basic design components?
- How do visitors react to the choices of exhibition objects in terms of quantity, attractiveness, appropriateness, etc.?

In the final analysis, the job of creating exhibitions that both satisfy the expectations of the public – are entertaining, attractive, and worthwhile – and yet provide educational opportunities – serve the public good and fulfill the museum mission – is the challenge that museums face today. Complacency is no longer an option. Evaluation, in its multiple forms, is a prime method for determining if the challenge is being met.

7

Storyline and text development

The storyline

The storyline is a compound document that serves design and production by
providing the framework upon which the educational content of the exhibition
hangs – a written blueprint for the exhibition. It is too narrow to consider the
storyline as simply a linear outline of the exhibition's flow of information.
Creating a storyline involves several elements. Each builds upon the preceding
one. The storyline consists of:

- a narrative document
- an outline of the exhibition
- a list of titles, sub-titles and text
- a list of collection objects

The process of storyline and text development begins at the point of origin for
an exhibition idea. The conception of an idea carries with it an assumption that
the conceiver has a notion, vaguely perhaps, of what the exhibition is to
contain and what it is about. As with most museum activities, objects are
usually central to the development of ideas. While it is possible that an idea
might arise that is not founded on collections, it is unlikely that it will entirely
neglect some point toward which the exhibition will be aimed.

At the beginning of an exhibition idea comes the need to determine how to
communicate its message: the interpretive strategy. This is the start of the
storyline process.

The development of interpretive strategies is a journey best embarked upon in
the company of others. There are few individuals who are able to generate and
deliver complex and complete orchestrations of information and imagery
single-handedly. Most benefit from the interchange of thoughts and vision
found in group activities such as brainstorming sessions.

A brainstorming meeting is not a formal affair. Indeed, it is usually better if it
is as informal as possible. The only structure needed is a comfortable place to
gather, a subject to focus upon, and someone to take notes. The basic idea is
to bandy an exhibition subject around between the participants so that

associations, suggestions, and relationships can flow freely. Many ideas will seem outlandish and impractical, but that works to generate new ways of thinking about a subject that will prove profitable. It is important that the brainstormers stay somewhere in the vicinity of the subject, but discussion, argument, and compromise are all appropriate.

The brainstorming session may include a wide variety of people. Staff members, community participants, and specialists may be involved in generating ideas. These individuals will have served their particular function in the process at that point, and the work will go on with a smaller group: the exhibition team. In some institutions, the exhibition team may be one or two persons, and in another, five or six. What is to be gained from the brainstorming sessions is a sense of direction for the interpretive thrust of the exhibition. If one brainstorming session is inconclusive, then another might be needed.

Meeting notes will often reveal patterns of interpretation or strategies emerging. Sometimes these are very familiar and at other times, new and unusual solutions for communicating ideas will be discovered. The exhibition team can then move into the next part of the storyline development by conducting meetings to discuss and establish the goals of the exhibition. This further refines the direction of interpretation. In addition, the audience or audiences to be targeted, their needs and expectations, and the methods of getting the information across need to be established clearly. All of these elements are essential if the effectiveness of the process and the exhibition are to be assessed (see Chapter 6, p. 91–102).

Beyond evaluation, however, the audience and exhibition goals and objectives are necessary for determining how best to address the exhibition subject. In the loop of interpretation shown in Figure 7.1 (adapted from an illustration in Candace Matelic's video "Successful Interpretive Planning"),[1] the message and channels must be decided upon and tests for suitability planned.

As the process continues, coupled with team meetings, the work of research must be ongoing. The curator or subject expert will be generating the narrative document based upon his or her knowledge and the collections, plus other available sources. A preliminary list of objects will emerge, usually containing more items than will be needed. The interactive process of meeting, researching, and refining will proceed until the narrative is done.

Once the narrative is completed, then the educator, designer, and curator can begin sifting the information for topical divisions and methods of communication. The educator will look at the narrative in terms of its content with a view toward translating that information into digestible bites. The designer will be developing the visual elements needed to attract and hold viewer attention so that the message will be transmitted. The curator will continue to work with the other team members to ensure informational accuracy and to provide collection care expertise.

From the deliberations will evolve two or more additional documents: an outline of the exhibition, and the exhibition design. Story boards, charts of information flow, and other similar aids can result as well.

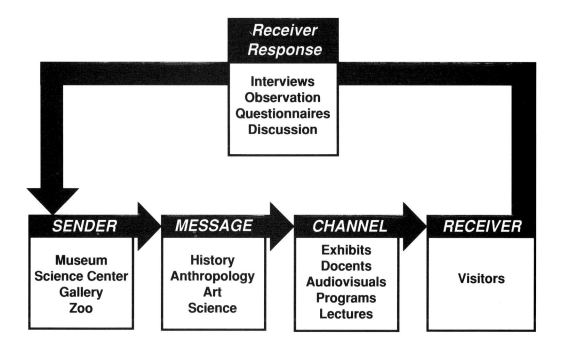

7.1 Interpretation loop

Once the outline and design are in hand, then a finalized listing of objects can be generated, and the titles, sub-titles, text copy, and labels can be produced. These elements make up the storyline document. With this master plan, the exhibition can be produced and executed.

Storyline and text development

- Concept of the exhibition
- Brainstorming sessions
- Exhibit team meetings:
    set goals and objectives
    determine audience
- Research is ongoing to produce the narrative document
- Research is ongoing to address collection management issues
- Curator and educator – produce outline of the exhibition
- Preliminary list of artifacts is submitted
- Team meetings:
    refining the message
    determining the approach(es) or channels for interpretation
    refining the list of collection objects

- Fleshing out the outline – storyboards and/or flowcharts of information
- Preliminary list of graphics
- Assigning collection objects to storyline segments
- Graphics assigned to storyline and artifacts
- Titles, sub-titles, and labels established and tested
- Designing the exhibition
- Establishing key exhibits, structures, shapes, traffic patterns, etc.
- Testing design elements for effectiveness and durability
- Writing text, labels, and other copy
- Testing text, labels, and copy for comprehension, terminology, etc.
- Production of the exhibition
- Function of the exhibition
- Terminating the exhibition
- Evaluating the design and storyline process and interpretive value

Storyline elements

Narrative document

The narrative is a manuscript for the exhibition. It is researched and written by the curatorial member of the exhibition team, and includes information about the exhibition subject extracted from the curator's knowledge of collections, object provenance, personal expertise, and any other identified resources he or she may have. The narrative will usually be or resemble a scholarly paper about the exhibition subject, much too wordy for label copy, and not always clearly delineating sections or topical divisions within the subject. In a sense, it is everything the curator feels should be known about the exhibition theme.

Normally, the narrative takes a good deal of time to generate because of the nature of research. During its development, the curator is honing his or her knowledge, discovering new information, and making associations not encountered before. These revelations should be included in the narrative if they apply to the exhibition. The development of an exhibition narrative may also lead the researcher into new lines of investigation and result in scholarly publications. The production of a narrative should be viewed as an intellectual pursuit equal to other such activities in academia.

The narrative is the first and foundational document of the storyline proper. The work of developing educational programs, designing exhibitions, and other such essential tasks wait upon the narrative as their guide. Once in hand, the other stages of exhibition development can take place. To attempt to generate a major exhibition without the storyline is to court confusion and disjointed interpretation.

Outline of the exhibition

This document will be formulated by the curator, educator, and designer of the team using the narrative, a preliminary list of objects to include, and the educational goals. They create a document which, in outline form, lists the major topics and sub-topics contained in the exhibition theme. This document is as detailed as is necessary to communicate clearly the type and levels of information and its direction of flow that will be reflected in the exhibition design.

For example, an exhibition on the ethnohistory of early humans in the New World might include topics such as the migrations of people, their technology, their lifestyles, their belief systems, the main resources upon which they relied, etc.

Example

    Title: Ethnohistory of the People of the Americas

    I   *Migrations*

    II *Technology*

    III *Lifestyles*

    IV *Beliefs*

    V *Resources*

Under the topic of technology, a series of sub-topics might address the techniques of container manufacture, food preparation, hunting tools, processing tools, toys, etc.

Example
  II Technology
    A. Making of tools
      1. container technologies
        a. methods of pot-making
        b. basketry techniques
        c. using animal resources
      2. weapons technologies
        a. projectile point production
        b. shaft production
        c. hardening techniques
    B. Food preparation
      1. gathering strategies
        a. seasonal cycles and resources
        b. types of animals and plants used
      2. processing tools and methods
        a. tools for processing plant materials
        b. tools for processing animal materials
      3. cooking and eating utensils
        a. cooking
        b. eating
        c. drinking

C. *Hunting*
1. *types of tools*
2. *passive strategies used*
   a. *cliff jumps*
   b. *pit traps*
   c. *canyon traps*
3. *active strategies used*
   a. *spears*
   b. *bows and arrows*

An outline will also include suggestions about the artifacts and objects to be used to illustrate the section, its general configuration for information flow, possible methods of addressing topics such as texts, audiovisuals, graphics, computers, and the like.

Example

II *Technology*
A. *Making of tools*
1. *container technologies*
   a. *methods of pot-making*
      (Holden film of modern Native American potter using ancient techniques; various styles of pottery produced by the native people: Accn #1975.25.1, #1942.150, #1991.25.1a)
   b. *basketry techniques*
      (diagrams of various stages of basket making: Accn #1975.25.35, #1987.42.78)

The outline is not intended to directly address the design or aesthetics of the exhibition, although the flow of information may well suggest specific layouts to be used, or colors having specific meanings within the subject context. Also, the educator will need to include requirements for educational programming. If the exhibition is to be used for school tours, then the educator will have to indicate where the tour groups will need space to gather near a docent, how many people a tour will consist of, and how other visitors will interact with the tours. If a demonstrator is to be part of the plan, then the space needs to be identified for that activity. Any such needs should be at the designer's fingertips when he or she begins laying out the gallery design. Hindsight is not useful except in planning the next exhibition.

To assist in developing the outline and to help determine how information is to be presented so that the visitors can absorb it, other sub-documents may be helpful, such as a storyboard or a flowchart of information.

- Storyboard: In some cases, a storyboard may be drawn up between the curator, educator, and designer so that communication is clear. This might consist of cards or placards and could include sketches. These are tacked to a bulletin board, wall, or a suitable flat surface in order of progression. The storyboard can be quite helpful in finalizing the content of an exhibition. By having people outside the team "read" the storyboard, a sort of pre-test for the success of the educational approach can be made. The storyboard provides an easily modified model of the exhibition content, allowing the process of development a certain degree of fluidity.

- Flowchart of information: A flowchart of information serves as an alternative or addition to the storyboard. This is a graphic showing the desired arrangement of information and its relation to the movement of the audience. This can be set up as a rough floorplan or simply a linear chart. If a floorplan is used, the planner must be careful to concentrate on the direction of information and not on designing the specific look of the exhibition. A flowchart is a planning tool, not a gallery design.

List of titles, sub-titles, and text

This document will often be included as part of the outline, but it should be the product of a team effort and some testing.

- Title Text: The title of the exhibition is an important piece of visual, written information. It sets the tone and parameters of the exhibition and serves as a major part of the curiosity "hook" needed to attract visitors into the gallery. The title should use visual language but avoid trite, cliche, or wordy verbiage.
- Sub-title Texts: These act as unifying visual and verbal guides through the exhibition. They serve the same purpose as newspaper headlines, giving in a few words the gist of each major topic and sub-topic. The sub-titles help the visitor, regardless of attention level, follow the flow of information and relationships between objects. They serve as markers to guide the visitor along through the exhibition subject. With the title and sub-titles alone, a patron should have a general idea of what the exhibition is about and the major ideas being presented.
- Label Texts: Text labels are often the most poorly thought out part of many exhibitions. Despite careful planning and execution of all other elements, an exhibition can suffer due to badly conceived and worded labels. In some cases the narrative is simply divided up and labels created using essentially unedited scholarly verbiage leaving the visitor intimidated or bored by the information. Labels are the heart of the educational content of the exhibition. They give the collection object the voice that it otherwise might not have, to speak of its own importance and uniqueness and tell its story. Labels are not intended to be the pages of a book, but rather they are presented in plain and concise language to reveal the important or relevant aspects of a segment of an exhibition or an object. The final development in the storyline sequence involves the formulation and refining of the text, group, and ID labels.

List of collection objects

The list of collection objects is not generated in a vacuum. It is carefully coordinated with the development of the narrative and outline so that all sets of documents then provide a complete picture of the final exhibition resources upon which the designer can draw in formulating the gallery plan and design. A preliminary, working list is generated by the curator while the narrative is being written. This first list will often include more objects than will finally be included in the exhibition. During the process of refining the narrative and creating the outline, the exhibition team will look over the preliminary list and, with the curator and collection manager's advice, select the final list. By the time the storyline is complete, the objects have been chosen and label copy has been written.

At this point, the designer's main function begins, or rather comes to fruition. Armed with all the information thus far generated and compiled, the designer should be able to configure the gallery to maximize the objects and educational mission of the exhibition.

Text preparation

Text comprises the written information presented for the interpretation of an exhibition. This includes the titles, text labels, object labels, and distributional materials. Titles serve as landmarks, identifying or signifying sections of the whole exhibition. Text labels serve as the principal in-depth educational resources for the exhibition. They explain, expound, and explore important aspects of the exhibition. Labels are identifiers and specifiers. They point out and clarify which object or objects are being emphasized. Distributional materials such as booklets and brochures, gallery notes, educational pamphlets, programs, and catalogs are means of presenting information that is too lengthy and complex for inclusion in the exhibition proper.

Text derives from the narrative, outline, storyboard/flowchart, and team interaction. Through the selective filters of the educator, designer, curator, and outside reviewers, the text gains clarity, simplicity, and readability. The end result should be a series of relatively short, concise blocks of copy that convey the salient points about the exhibition subject without getting bogged down in jargon, cliche, or triteness. A rule-of-thumb often cited is no more than 75 ± 5 words in a block of textual information. It is fundamentally important that text copy be written with the receiver (target audience) in mind and not as a forum for the verbal virtuosity of the staff (unless, of course, the audience happens to be other scholars).

To expand on each level of written or verbal information (since audio and other means can be used as "labeling" mechanisms), text may be considered in six levels:

- title signs
- sub-titles
- introductory text
- group texts
- object labels
- distributional materials

110

These constitute the basic divisions of verbal information in most exhibition schemes. The names of the divisions may be different depending upon the source, but the functions are essentially the same. In some cases, combinations of these elements may be used rather than each level being clearly separated from the others.

Levels of written information

- Title signs.
- Subtitle signs or sub-headings – section headers.
- Introductory text – statement of exhibition rationale.
- Group texts – labels for groupings of objects.
- Object labels – tags for individual collection items.
- Distributional materials – gallery notes, brochures, catalogs.

Title signs

Title signs as visual elements are important for stating just what the exhibition is about. They serve as minimal information communicators and as wayfinders. Typically, titles are short, usually no more than ten, and often only one or two words long. They are normally placed at the entrances to galleries announcing the exhibition to be found there. They use large-size lettering as a rule, are intentionally eye-catching, and are often placed well above eye-level to attract attention.

The informational content of titles is much the same as the masthead of a newspaper. It serves to thematically orient the viewer without imparting a great deal of information about the exhibition subject matter. The intent is also to fire the imagination and set a mood. Design is far more important than content. That is not to say that titles should be poorly thought out and are not important. On the contrary, they are essential in terms of attracting and holding attention and introducing the exhibition theme to the visitor.

Clever turns of phrase, familiar quotes or partial quotes, and other such verbal devices are employed in titles. Caution should be exercised to avoid overusing cliche or trite phrases. Bright colors are commonly used to attract attention and trigger moods. Titles are also indicators of acceptable behavior. Those that are verbally subdued, presented in muted colors, and arranged in regular patterns indicate that the appropriate behavior is to view the exhibition quietly. Bright, explosive colors, exaggerated arrangements of letters, and vibrant imagery tell the visitor to expect a lively, active experience.

Title signs

- Large panel size and imposing print.
- Short, 1–10 words.
- Attention grabbing.
- Thematically oriented – information content is superficial.
- Design over content.
- Mood setting (comic, serious, controversial, elegant, etc.).

Sub-title or sub-heading signs

Sub-title signs are the next step up in information content. They are typically smaller in typesize and longer – up to twenty words – than titles, but are still large enough to read at a distance. These correspond to the headlines in a newspaper. They help to narrow the focus within a particular segment of the exhibition gallery by addressing the topic covered there. It should be possible by reading the title and sub-titles to come away with a general sense of the exhibition's subject and content.

Sub-titles commonly use familiar phrases and plays on words to fire the visitor's imagination, and to prepare him or her to address the exhibition section information. "The Desert: A Desolate Land . . . Teeming with Life," or "Electricity . . . Exciting Electrons" are examples of sectional sub-titles. Contrast, alliteration, and metaphor are used to stimulate intellectual curiosity. The visual appeal of sub-titles is important, but readability is also necessary. Whereas a title sign might require some interpretation on the patron's part to decipher, the sub-titles should be clear at a glance.

Sub-title (section headings) signs

- Longer than titles – 10–20 words.
- Large; easy to read from a distance.
- Content more focused and informational.
- Topic oriented.
- Design and content about equal.

Introductory text

At a more complex level of information delivery stand the text labels. Of these, the introductory label plays a particularly significant role. It presents the first sizable block of information to the visitor, setting the pattern of textual presentation for the rest of the exhibition. The introductory text contains more words and gives the visitor a quick sense of the major concepts in the exhibition. Usually, the introductory label will be placed on a panel with or near the title sign, or will at least appear close to the beginning of the exhibition. It is an explanatory, unifying statement that presents the rationale for the exhibition.

The general rule of thumb for blocks of text is that they should be no longer than 75 words, since the average visitor will not read more than that. This, however, depends a great deal on how clearly and simply the text is written, and how legible it appears. If information is written in a lively, visually oriented style that captures the reader's interest, more words are possible. If the text is limited to short, concise paragraphs, then up to 200 words can be included.

In multiple-paragraph texts the rule of 75 words should be applied to paragraph length. Spacing between the paragraphs should be sufficient to give an open, uncluttered appearance to the copy. This will enhance its visual appeal. Also, in text blocks which are the length of introductory labels, the typesize should be large enough for easy reading; the typestyle should be highly legible. Sans serif typestyles such as Helvetica, Futura, and Avant Garde fulfill these requirements, as do serif texts such as Times-Roman and Garamond. Typesizes of 18–36 points are generally advisable. Positive text – black text on white background – is better for longer labels because it is less fatiguing to the eyes.

Introductory text

- **Longer – 50–200 words divided into succinct, concise paragraphs about 75 words in length.**
- **Usually located near the entry to the exhibition.**
- **Explanatory – relates the rationale for the exhibition; a unifying statement.**
- **Introduces major concepts within the exhibition.**

Group texts

Like introductory texts, group texts are a higher level of information transfer. The distinction is that group texts are used to introduce and interpret segments within the exhibition. Again the 75-word rule applies, but up to 150 words are practical if paragraph breaks are used and text size and style are conducive to easy reading.

The purpose of the group text is to unify a particular group of objects or data conceptually. Often the group text will accompany sub-titles, or will begin with a short title, sometimes called a "kicker." This is a short title for the group text that attracts attention by exciting interest in much the same way as a sub-title identifies and points to the exhibition section.

Group texts typically require the greatest effort to read since they contain a major portion of the verbal interpretive message. For this reason, they need to be well thought out and succinctly phrased to avoid losing the visitor's attention.

Group texts

- 75–150 words in length.
- Associated with groupings of objects or serve as section texts.
- Sometimes begin with a "kicker" or heading.
- Unifies grouping conceptually.
- Informative, interpretive.

Object labels

The object label is a critical element in the interpretive flow of information. It provides the visitor with details about specific collection items. The object label answers a basic question: "What is it?" Although object labels can be structured in many ways, with varied appearances, there are essentially two types: captions and identity tags.

A caption is a small text block concerning one particular object (or a few very closely related objects). It usually contains detailed information about the object, providing in-depth commentary. Normally, the 75-word rule is in effect and typestyle is kept conservative for legibility's sake. Typesize is generally between 12 and 24 points in height to allow the text to be read easily. The main consideration is to provide legibility without having the label become visually competitive with the object.

The identity tag or ID label is a set of descriptive data about an object. It provides only basic facts such as the name or title of the object, its maker or origin, the material the object is made of, pertinent dates, collection or catalog numbers, and other relevant data. The ID label is probably the most familiar and simplest form of textual material in exhibitions. In many museums, aside from the title sign and an introductory panel, the identity tag will be the only information presented with the individual objects.

It is important that object labels be as well thought through as the other textual materials in a gallery. It is often a temptation to make ID labels and captions as quickly as possible, and as the last item in the production schedule. However, these bits of information strongly impact the visitor's perception of the exhibition as a whole. Professionally produced, well-written labels lend the exhibition an air of credibility and completeness. To scrimp on time or materials in producing object labels is a mistake.

```
Object labels
● Captions
   Interpretive, informative
   Specific to an object or small group
   No more than 75 words
● ID labels
   Contain basic facts
   Give objects a name
```

Distributed materials

Distributed materials can be any one of a variety of publications. They may be anything from exhibition catalogs or gallery notes to computer print-outs from an interactive exhibition. The reasons for auxiliary printed materials are varied as well. They may be produced to simply document the exhibition as an event, to proffer more information about the exhibition subject, to nurture an interest in further learning engendered by the exhibition, to provide a tangible "souvenir" of having attended the exhibition, and for many other reasons.

Often the informational content of an exhibition (the narrative) is either too long, too esoteric, or otherwise inappropriate to be contained within the exhibition design *in toto*. Distributed materials are an ideal outlet for such information. In some cases, due to audience attention span, numbers of visitors, lack of space, or other limiting factors, gallery notes or brochures provide the detailed auxiliary information deemed important but not essential to the actual exhibition storyline. Also, printed matter provides excellent channels for expanding upon the exhibition subject matter.

Usually, distributed materials such as gallery notes and brochures are calculated more for intellectual than for visual appeal. That is, although a brochure may be well designed and visually pleasing, it will usually emphasize information over images. This allows such publications to explore in depth certain facets of the exhibition subject matter. Philosophical connections which are difficult to communicate in the principally visual, imagery-oriented environment of the gallery can be explored with handouts. This opens up a whole realm of educational possibilities.

Distributed materials are produced in many lengths and complexities. For those intended to be given as handouts in the galleries, a single sheet or folded pamphlet is advisable. The important factor is that they be easily portable, and pocket-able. If handouts are clumsy and bulky, they will generally end up being discarded somewhere within the museum, often in another exhibition gallery. Since the primary rationale behind making printed materials available is the intent to foster long-term interest in the museum and its exhibitions, designing well-thought-out, professionally produced materials needs careful attention.

Another way of approaching distributed materials is to place them in the visitor's hand for the duration of the visit and then request that they be returned for others to use later. In exhibitions with a large quantity of items, a numbering system is often used to identify individual objects. A returnable, laminated card or pamplet can replace lengthy, clumsy labels. Since the information is of little use to the viewer without the objects to look at, this strategy works nicely. This same principle applies to portable audio devices for use in the galleries. Copies of the information or tapes can be sold in the museum shop.

Distributed materials

- Optional – give away materials, contain information not necessary to the exhibition but still valuable.
- Targeted – aimed at the interested visitor.
- Information intensive – content over style; explores philosophical concepts.
- Longer – unlimited text.
- Portable – easy to carry; pocket-able.

Guidelines for writing effective text

Writing text for an exhibition is not as simple as telling the visitor everything you know about a subject. Care must be taken to utilize the audience's recognition of what is familiar or intriguing to them as a "hook" or basis upon which to attach new information. To do this, it is important to know what makes good text successful and what leads to failure. Creative and journalistic writing are entire subjects in themselves, requiring years of education and experience to master. It is not the author's intent to cover the nuances of those fields in this book. However, some general guidelines may be useful in developing effective text for exhibitions.

To prepare text properly, an understanding of the nature of the reader is required. There are some generalizations that can be helpful guides but not fast rules. Although it depends greatly on the community, an average reading level is that achieved by a student at about 13–14 years of age. If the average level is higher or lower than this, it is important to target the actual reading ability of the audience.

People will only make the effort to read what they find interesting and easy to understand. The objects in the exhibition are the primary focus of attention. The text that accompanies and explains them must answer questions posed by people viewing the objects. Most people are pleasant and uncomplaining and will appreciate whatever is presented for their benefit. They will also tend to believe what they read. Since most will not be very knowledgeable about the exhibition subject, they will be willing to be informed and will trust the museum to provide them with accurate information.

> *Common pitfalls to avoid in producing exhibition text*
> - Text too long and wordy.
> - Text too technical and uses too much jargon. "Reads like a textbook."
> - Text is boring. It contains inappropriate or esoteric information.
> - Bad editing and proofreading allow spelling and grammatical errors that are distracting and detract from credibility.
> - Lettering too small or contains too many flourishes.
> - Print is hard to read or illegible due to poor production techniques.
> - Text design is poor. Improper use of colors or poor contrast.
> - Text is poorly placed. It is too high or low, is hard to find, or poorly lit.

To communicate effectively in an exhibition setting, text needs to be pertinent and direct. There is not a great deal of latitude for personal or creative writing styles. The content of the textual materials should answer questions or pose new ones. It should use language that is familiar to the audience. The use of jargon or technical terminology is generally an impediment to effective reading.

At first glance, textual material should arrest attention. A traditional method of accomplishing this effect is to make the first letter of a copy block larger than the body text – a "drop cap." Other methods involve placing a small graphic near the beginning of the first line, or making the first line of copy bold or italic. The visual appeal of the text is a matter of design with many good solutions.

The informational impact of the text is also of major concern. No matter how attractive the graphic nature of lettering may be, it is content and meaning that hold interest. The first sentence of a text block should use wording that both attracts and holds attention. If a reader becomes hooked by a tantalizing initial sentence, he or she is more likely to continue reading the information. Also, if interest is aroused, then assimilation of meaning is enhanced.

A way to capture interest in the textual material is to appeal to the whole thinking process in humans. Since the left brain is the analytical center and the right brain is the imagery processor, appealing to both will be most effective (see Chapter 2, p. 30). The right brain is the expert at making a whole picture out of the bits and pieces of the puzzle (*pars pro toto*). Suggestions and associations are effective at communicating a great deal more information than is actually written. If done correctly and accurately, exploiting this facility of the brain can impart information more clearly and rapidly than the presentation of bare facts.

Adding interest to text

- Ask questions. Stimulate imagination and curiosity. Be sure to answer the questions somewhere in the exhibition.
- Use familiar language.
- Use easily recognized quotations to support ideas.
- Compare the familiar with the unfamiliar; analogy.
- Reference common human experiences.
- Interaction. Give instructions. Ask or tell the reader to do or look for something. People prefer to be involved.
- Use interesting or intriguing word pictures.
- Parody familiar phrases or wording such as popular advertising.

For example, a word picture that compares the flow of electricity in a copper wire with the flow of water through a garden hose can be far more effective at communicating basic information about electricity than simply stating the factual information about the movement of electrons. This is because most people will be familiar with water and hoses, whereas electricity is an invisible, mysterious force. Analogies, fables, parables, similes, metaphor, and other such literary devices, used with discretion, can enhance the success of textual communication tremendously. There is a caution, however. The same devices can be overdone. Unless they are used carefully with a great deal of thought about what the verbal pictures actually say, they can impart erroneous as easily as correct information.

To summarize, here are some guidelines for effective writing:[2]

- Use visual language having observable interpretations and facts. Appeal to the visual thinking process (right brain oriented thinking).
- Use active verbs and interesting words. Read the copy aloud for its sound.
- Keep sentences short and concise – less than 25 words.
- Use variety and avoid overuse of "to be" verbs.
- Get to the point. Make the lead sentence important.
- Use conversational language. Avoid jargon or esoteric terminology.
- Construct concise sentences. Use a vigorous style; avoid meaningless words such as "rather," "very," and "little."
- Remove unnecessary detail. Avoid lots of adverbs and adjectives.
- Avoid abstractions. Relate to events and relationships, not ideas and dry facts; draw word pictures.

Evaluative criteria for good text
- Conveys intended message accurately and succinctly.
- Readable – uses visual language.
- Legible – easy to decipher.
- Attention-grabbing, both visually and verbally.
- Interesting – provides information that the visitor wants to learn.

Not all conditions are suitable or advisable for written text. Each museum must assess its audiences and determine how best to develop text-based communication. Depending upon text as the sole means of interpretation may lead to ineffective communication. Some exhibitions are oriented more toward activities using objects than toward the objects themselves. In living history museums, first- or third-person interpretation by a docent is frequently more effective than labeling. In art museums, labeling may be kept minimal if docent-led tours are employed. The spoken message can often communicate better than textual materials.

Younger children do not have well-developed analytical skills. Brain activity is not fully developed and participatory learning is more effective than written communication. Again, interpretation by a tour guide or teacher coupled with hands-on activity is far more effective than text and labels. In many children's museums, written material is more often targeted at the accompanying adult than at the child. The adult will normally want to use the textual information as a basis for instructing his or her charges. The language, then, needs to be aimed toward the child's viewpoint and kept at an elementary level.

Typography and production methods

Textual materials in exhibitions must be "designed" just like any other exhibition element. When referring to text, however, design has at least two distinct meanings. One meaning refers to the deliberate effort made to "construct" text which is interesting, informative, and appropriate for the exhibition subject. In this sense, "design" relates to content, writing style, grammar, and other textual concerns already covered.

The other meaning of design in text relates to the visual, physical appearance and arrangement of graphic elements such as letters, sentences, paragraphs, and other type-specific characteristics. In this sense, the design is tied to a more traditional design activity: typography.

> Webster's *New World Dictionary* defines typography as "the arrangement, style, or general appearance of matter printed from type."

The visual appearance of text is important. A block of text that is long and complex will probably be ignored. People are much more interested in the objects than the words. The legibility of the text is critical. Lettering should be of a size and type that is easy to read for the elderly as well as the young.

There are several considerations with which the type designer is chiefly concerned. They are legibility, contrast, structure, and method. Legibility refers to the choice of font and size of type. Contrast relates to the lightness or darkness of print, relative sizes of type, and style of font. Structure refers to how the text is arranged, ordered, and modified. Method has to do with the actual production of the text for presentation. In each of these four aspects, there are rules of thumb, warnings, or needs to be addressed.

Legibility

The viewing distance for normal reading, such as for a book, is 12–15 in. (30.5–38.1 cm) for text set in 8–10 point type. In an exhibition environment, the visitor is usually further from the text – 24–48 in. (60.9–121.9 cm). Increasing that distance in the above size ranges will make text harder to read. Increasing the size of text will increase the distance from which it can be read comfortably. This translates into a "standard" for group text, generally viewed from 2–3 ft (60–90 cm), as a range of 24–36 point type, and for individual labels, 14–24 point type.

Another aspect of legibility revolves around an average adult reading speed of 250–300 words per minute.[3] The first-glance attention span of a visitor is only a few seconds – 20 at best. If the text appears complex or long, the visitor will not stay to read it. If the text is not clear and legible, reading speed suffers, attention wanders, and interest is quickly lost.

In terms of typefaces or typestyles, the more letters deviate from basic block lettering, the more difficult they become to read. Hence, serif fonts are slightly more difficult to decipher than sans serif types. Fonts with exaggerated serifs or curlicues and those that are elongated or compressed are more difficult to read.

If properly organized, legible and interesting, the 75–150-word rule is reasonable for copy length. It is wise to admit that text that is difficult or appears difficult to understand, no matter how artistically arranged or well written, will be ignored. If the message is important, keep it short and to the point.

Contrast

In the area of contrast, dark print against a light background is easiest to read and is kinder to the optic nerves than light on dark. In limited use, such as for titles and sub-titles, light on dark is useful, attention-grabbing, and visually striking. For larger blocks of text, it is fatiguing to look at and will lead to blurring vision. A rule of thumb is to limit light against dark print to around 20 words.

Using transparencies that are lit from behind is a commonly used technique for text display. It is especially popular in low light settings. However, back-lighting has a similar effect to light on dark printing – it makes reading more difficult and physically fatiguing to the eyes. Again, limited to use as a visual accent, such as in sub-titles and wayfinders, back-lit text is valuable. For group texts, it should be avoided in favor of front-lit, dark on light type. The 20-word rule is applicable here as well.

Another popular contrast is the use of mixed typestyles. These create interest and are a useful way of separating and emphasizing portions of a block of text. However, using too many typestyles in one set of text creates visual confusion. More will be said about the different styles of text but a rule of thumb is to use fonts that are dramatically dissimilar and limit their use to two or three styles within one block.

One less concrete aspect of typestyle choice is the mood or emotional impact it invokes. Busy typefaces containing exaggerated serifs and flourishes are visually confusing and difficult to decipher. Sans serif types read as cool, unemotional, or clinical. These are useful for presenting factual information. Serif and cursive typefaces are more friendly and familiar. Simple serif typefaces such as are used in newspapers and books evoke the emotional response of familiarity.

Contrast

- **Keep light against dark type to a minimum. Use for titles and subtitles in large type sizes. The 20-word rule applies.**
- **Keep back-lit copy to a minimum. Use for accents such as sub-titles and wayfinders. The 20-word rule applies.**
- **Mix typefaces such as serif and sans serif, but limit mixing to one or two diverse styles. Do not mix similar typestyles.**

Structure

Structure is a complex topic. It concerns the physical arrangement of the text. Decisions about margins, length of line, shape of the text block, and special type treatments come under this heading.

Margins are basically simple. Text is either lined up along one side of the page or the other, or both, or neither. When the alignment is on the left side, it is called justified left or ragged right text. When aligned on the right side, the terms are justified right or ragged left. If the type is aligned so that it is even on both the right and the left, it is referred to as being justified text. When the margins are ragged, but the text is aligned so that each line is centered, it is called centered text. For short line length, ragged right is generally best. Text in columns often works well in a justified format, but unless adjustments can be made, justified text often contains uneven spacing.

Around AD 1200, the Anasazi (ancestors of the Puebloan peoples) engaged in complex and widespread migrations. By AD 1400, if not earlier, the Athapaskans were moving down the Rocky Mountain chain on the Western Plains. On the Southern Plains the Antelope Creek people lived along the Canadian River in slab-lined houses and practiced agriculture. While further south, unnamed semi-nomadic hunter-gatherers continued their bison-hunting ways on seasonal rounds across the Plains.

7.2 Justified left (ragged right)

Around AD 1200, the Anasazi (ancestors of the Puebloan peoples) engaged in complex and widespread migrations. By AD 1400, if not earlier, the Athapaskans were moving down the Rocky Mountain chain on the Western Plains. On the Southern Plains the Antelope Creek people lived along the Canadian River in slab-lined houses and practiced agriculture. While further south, unnamed semi-nomadic hunter-gatherers continued their bison-hunting ways on seasonal rounds across the Plains.

7.3 Justified right (ragged left)

Around AD 1200, the Anasazi (ancestors of the Puebloan peoples) engaged in complex and widespread migrations. By AD 1400, if not earlier, the Athapaskans were moving down the Rocky Mountain chain on the Western Plains. On the Southern Plains the Antelope Creek people lived along the Canadian River in slab-lined houses and practiced agriculture. While further south, unnamed semi-nomadic hunter-gatherers continued their bison-hunting ways on seasonal rounds across the Plains.

7.4 Justified text

Around AD 1200, the Anasazi (ancestors of the Puebloan peoples) engaged in complex and widespread migrations. By AD 1400, if not earlier, the Athapaskans were moving down the Rocky Mountain chain on the Western Plains. On the Southern Plains the Antelope Creek people lived along the Canadian River in slab-lined houses and practiced agriculture. While further south, unnamed semi-nomadic hunter-gatherers continued their bison-hunting ways on seasonal rounds across the Plains.

7.5 Centered text

Length of line and shape of text are related considerations. Text can be organized into generally vertical, square, round, horizontal, or shaped formats. Deciding how the text is to be shaped then depends on its placement and use in the exhibition.

Around AD 1200, the Anasazi (ancestors of the Puebloan peoples) engaged in complex and widespread migrations. By AD 1400, if not earlier, the Athapaskans were moving down the Rocky Mountain chain on the Western Plains. On the Southern Plains the Antelope Creek people lived along the Canadian River in slab-lined houses and practiced agriculture. While further south, unnamed semi-nomadic hunter-gatherers continued their bison-hunting ways on seasonal rounds across the Plains.

7.6 Horizontally oriented text block

Around AD 1200, the Anasazi (ancestors of the Puebloan peoples) engaged in complex and widespread migrations. By AD 1400, if not earlier, the Athapaskans were moving down the Rocky Mountain chain on the Western Plains. On the Southern Plains the Antelope Creek people lived along the Canadian River in slab-lined houses and practiced agriculture. While further south, unnamed semi-nomadic hunter-gatherers continued their bison-hunting ways on seasonal rounds across the Plains.

7.7 Vertically oriented text block

Italicizing, bolding, underlining, expanding or compressing text are other options available in typography. These are generally utilized for specific grammatical or stylistic reasons. However, visual impact can be important too. When expanding or compressing text, the terms "kerning" and "leading" (as in the metal lead) are often encountered. Kerning refers to the spacing between letters, and leading refers to spaces between lines of text.

Around AD 1200, the Anasazi (ancestors of the Puebloan peoples) engaged in
complex and widespread migrations. By AD 1400, if not earlier, the Athapaskans were moving
down the Rocky Mountain chain on the Western Plains. On the
Southern Plains the Antelope Creek people lived along the Canadian River in
slab-lined houses and practiced agriculture. While further south, unnamed
semi-nomadic hunter-gatherers continued their bison-hunting ways on seasonal rounds across the
Plains.

7.8 Italicized text

Around AD 1200, the Anasazi (ancestors of the Puebloan peoples) engaged in
complex and widespread migrations. By AD 1400, if not earlier, the Athapaskans were moving
down the Rocky Mountain chain on the Western Plains. On the
Southern Plains the Antelope Creek people lived along the Canadian River in
slab-lined houses and practiced agriculture. While further south, unnamed
semi-nomadic hunter-gatherers continued their bison-hunting ways on seasonal rounds
across the Plains.

7.9 Bold text

Around AD 1200, the Anasazi (ancestors of the Puebloan peoples) engaged in
complex and widespread migrations. By AD 1400, if not earlier, the Athapaskans were
moving down the Rocky Mountain chain on the Western Plains. On the
Southern Plains the Antelope Creek people lived along the Canadian River in
slab-lined houses and practiced agriculture. While further south, unnamed
semi-nomadic hunter-gatherers continued their bison-hunting ways on seasonal rounds
across the Plains.

7.10 Underlined text

124

Around AD 1200, the Anasazi (ancestors of the Puebloan peoples) engaged in complex and widespread migrations. By AD 1400, if not earlier, the Athapaskans were moving down the Rocky Mountain chain on the Western Plains. On the Southern Plains the Antelope Creek people lived along the Canadian River in slab-lined houses and practiced agriculture. While further south, unnamed semi-nomadic hunter-gatherers continued their bison-hunting ways on seasonal rounds across the Plains.

7.11 Expanded text

Around AD 1200, the Anasazi (ancestors of the Puebloan peoples) engaged in complex and widespread migrations. By AD 1400, if not earlier, the Athapaskans were moving down the Rocky Mountain chain on the Western Plains. On the Southern Plains the Antelope Creek people lived along the Canadian River in slab-lined houses and practiced agriculture. While further south, unnamed semi-nomadic hunter-gatherers continued their bison-hunting ways on seasonal rounds across the Plains.

7.12 Condensed text

Production methods

Available production technology dictates what is possible as far as legibility, contrast, and structure are concerned. Letters can be produced in many ways. Silk screening, computerized systems, off-set printing, commercially available transfer letters, projecting and hand painting, and using ceramic and plastic letters are but a few of the many methods. Printing and graphic production techniques vary greatly in the image resolution, the surface requirements, the amount of machinery needed, and the number of steps in the process. Some methods are too costly to be produced in-house. Others require a great deal of time or years of experience to master.

The computer has been one of the major innovations in the area of typesetting. The speed of setting type and the flexibility to preview many different typestyles and sizes in a variety of different treatments allows the designer to select the arrangement best suited to the purpose. It is possible, if he or she is so inclined, for a designer to create his or her own typestyles for specific uses. Also, commercially available types are able to be distorted, stretched, or enhanced with many computer programs to create different appearances for standard typestyles.

Computerized systems that produce commercial quality printing are becoming increasingly affordable. These systems can print routed or "die-cut" lettering in a wide range of sizes and styles. They can also produce graphic images other than lettering just as easily. In-house printing devices such as laser and bubble-jet printers are also becoming available with dot resolutions that rival the commercial machines.

While some more traditional technologies are still viable, the computer is replacing or enhancing many of them. Some of the more familiar methods of graphic production are being improved by the addition of computer capabilities. Silk screening is still widely used to produce title signs, large blocks of text, and detailed images such as maps and diagrams. The computer can be used to create the positive or negative images from which the screens are made. Off-set printing is still much in use in producing brochures, gallery guides and other such distributed materials, but the computer is being used to prepare the camera-ready artwork from which printing is accomplished. In the area of preparing text for group and object labels, the computer is making significant inroads for many museums and has replaced other methods in some. The trend toward automation of text production will likely continue, and will improve the capabilities of production staffs.

Type specifications

When discussing type and communicating preferences to commercial printers about style, certain terms are commonly used. Words like font, serif, leading, kerning, enlargement, descenders, ascenders, points, bolding and italics are part of the typesetting jargon. Even though much of the future of typesetting will lie in the hands of the museum staff, there will probably continue to be a need to utilize the services of commercial firms for some printing jobs. It is wise to be familiar with the terminology used.

What is a "font?" Is it different from or the same as a "typeface" or "typestyle"? Typeface and typestyle are synonymous. They refer to the particular style or design of a set of letters. Typestyles are named for identification, often quite imaginatively. Avant Garde, Garamond, Century, Bookman, Times, Roman, Palatino, Futura, Koloss, Tinker, and Univers 55 are but a few of the thousands of typestyles available. They are named by their designer, or the appellations are derived from common usage and tradition.

Font, on the other hand, refers to the complete set of characters (capitals and lower case), sizes, numbers, treatments (italics, bold, etc.), and symbols (&, %, !, ?, etc.) within a particular typestyle. Often the typestyle and font are used interchangeably, but there is a true difference. When one purchases a font, it should include all of the items above.

Serif and sans serif typestyles are commonly used terms. The serif is the "tail," "tab," or "flag" that appears on the extremities of letters within a serif typeface. Many of the most familiar typestyles are serif types. Times-Roman, Century, Garamond, New York, and Palatino are examples of common serif types. These are "friendly" typestyles, often used in newsprint, books, and other forms of printed matter read daily.

126

Around AD 1200, the Anasazi (ancestors of the Puebloan peoples) engaged in complex and widespread migrations. By AD 1400, if not earlier, the Athapaskans were moving down the Rocky Mountain chain on the Western Plains. On the Southern Plains the Antelope Creek people lived along the Canadian River in slab-lined houses and practiced agriculture. While further south, unnamed semi-nomadic hunter-gatherers continued their bison-hunting ways on seasonal rounds across the Plains.

7.13 Times-Roman typestyle

The small word "sans" means "without." A sans serif typeface is one without serifs. Common examples of these fonts are Helvetica and Futura. These are sometimes referred to as block type. They are thought of as being technical and scientific, or unemotional. Their great advantage is their legibility due to their clean lines and lack of flourish.

Around AD 1200, the Anasazi (ancestors of the Puebloan peoples) engaged in complex and widespread migrations. By AD 1400, if not earlier, the Athapaskans were moving down the Rocky Mountain chain on the Western Plains. On the Southern Plains the Antelope Creek people lived along the Canadian River in slab-lined houses and practiced agriculture. While further south, unnamed semi-nomadic hunter-gatherers continued their bison-hunting ways on seasonal rounds across the Plains.

7.14 Helvetica typestyle

Another common typestyle is cursive. Typefaces that have a flowing appearance, often with letters connected to each other by tails or flourishes in imitation of handwriting, are cursives. A true cursive typestyle has connected letters, but some computer typefaces are "pseudo-cursive," meaning they have the flowing appearance but the characters are distinct and unconnected. These typestyles are friendly, informal, and often appear elegant. Zapf Chancery is an example of this type.

Around AD 1200, the Anasazi (ancestors of the Puebloan peoples) engaged in complex and widespread migrations. By AD 1400, if not earlier, the Athapaskans were moving down the Rocky Mountain chain on the Western Plains. On the Southern Plains the Antelope Creek people lived along the Canadian River in slab-lined houses and practiced agriculture. While further south, unnamed semi-nomadic hunter-gatherers continued their bison-hunting ways on seasonal rounds across the Plains.

7.15 Zapf Chancery typestyle

Many typestyles are speciality fonts and have limited application, not falling easily into any one category. Time and preference have left only a few that are simple and legible enough to be used for general text purposes, but even those few provide a great deal of variety in design.

Around AD 1200, the Anasazi (ancestors of the Puebloan peoples) engaged in complex and widespread migrations. By AD 1400, if not earlier, the Athapaskans were moving down the Rocky Mountain chain on the Western Plains. On the Southern Plains the Antelope Creek people lived along the Canadian River in slab-lined houses and practiced agriculture. While further south, unnamed semi-nomadic hunter-gatherers continued their bison-hunting ways on seasonal rounds across the Plains.

7.16 Old English typestyle

Points or point size are terms common to typography. A point is a measurement unit equal to about 0.0138 in. (0.035 cm). There are 72 points per inch (2.54 cm). A pica is a term for 12 points equal to one sixth of an inch. Type sizes are usually given in points. There have been many systems of measurement developed over the history of typesetting. Terms such as agates and picas are still used by some, but without getting into the confusing jungle of jargon, the term point has become a standard in most discussion of print size and for computer programs used in typesetting.

The size of type is figured from an imaginary baseline upon which the letters sit and includes both ascenders (capitals and tall letters) and descenders (letters with tails or flourishes such as the "g" and "y"). The combined height of ascenders and descenders is the point size of the type. The "H" measurement is the height of the capital letters from the baseline. The "x" height is the average lower case letter without ascenders or descenders.

Spacing refers to the distance between letters in text. On the manual typewriter, each letter is given the same space on the page. The result is the familiar crowded "w" and the isolated "i." Good typography, however, adjusts the spacing to produce an even appearance in the type. Curved letters such as "O" and "p" need less space than letters such as "l" and "i." Adjustments are made to accommodate these differences. The spaces become relative or proportional to the letters themselves.

Another aspect of spacing is the distance between words. This is usually the width of the letter "e" in the font, called the "e" width. Normally, word spacing is about equal throughout the copy. Too much distance gives an appearance of disjointedness; too little is crowded and confusing. Spacing is handled automatically with many computerized typesetting systems, but most will also allow for custom kerning or spacing.

A foolish consistency is the hobgoblin of litte minds.–RWE–
Playbill 24 pt.

A foolish consistency is the hobgoblin of litte minds.—RWE—
Bauhaus 93 12 pt.

A foolish consistency is the hobgoblin of litte minds.—RWE—
Old English 14 pt.

A foolish consistency is the hobgoblin of litte
minds.—RWE—Braggadocio 12 pt.

A foolish consistency is the hobgoblin of litte minds.—RWE—
Hobo 12 pt.

A foolish consistency is the hobgoblin of litte minds.—RWE—
Mistral 18 pt.

A foolish consistency is the hobgoblin of litte minds.—RWE—Snell
Roundhand 12 pt.

A FOOLISH CONSISTENCY IS THE HOBGOBLIN OF LITTE MINDS.—
RWE—STENCIL 12 PT.

A foolish consistency is the hobgoblin of litte minds.——RWE——Runic MT Condensed 18 pt.

7.17 Examples of specialty typestyles

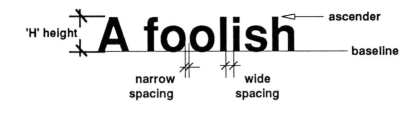

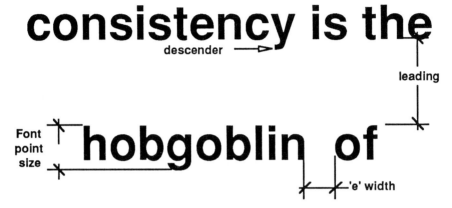

7.18 Typographic terms

Leading is a term used to describe the distance between lines of type. When type was set by hand, the space between the lines was created by a strip of the metal lead. Leading is a term still used today. The normal amount of "lead" between lines of type is 2 points greater than the point size of the type. This leaves adequate room for the lines to remain distinct without being difficult to read as a unit.

Style also refers to such treatments of text as italics, underlining, and bolding. Bold and demi are meant to indicate the strength or heaviness of the line in a character. Bold is the densest and strongest. Demi is somewhere between bold and plain text.

In typesetting, the question of enlargement or reduction will arise. The terms "blow-up" or "blow-down" are in reference to the enlargement–reduction process. In general, for a given point size, 300 percent enlargement is the maximum that will hold resolution well. A 50 percent reduction will increase resolution of an image, but will reduce legibility. To calculate percentages for typesize changes, the following simple formulae work if a percentage/scale device is not on hand:

$$\text{Enlargement formula: } (A/D) \times 100 = \%$$
$$\text{Reduction formula: } (D/A) \times 100 = \%$$
$$A = \text{actual size}$$
$$D = \text{desired size}$$

7.19 Enlargement/reduction formulae

Conclusions

Both the design of the writing in exhibition texts and the appearance of the lettering and symbols used have significant impact on the effectiveness of communication.

The storyline provides the framework upon which to build the exhibition's message. It acts like the animator's storyboard by providing the raw material for producing the finished work. The storyline can no more be ignored or omitted than can the plot of a book. Without the storyline, planning is chaotic and ineffectual.

It is through the cooperation of the subject expert, the designer, and the educator that the correct messages and channels are chosen to educate and enlighten the public who expect and deserve the best.

The writing that the visitor encounters in the exhibition environment must meet his or her needs. The museum is not a forum for verbal virtuosity. It is a place where the uninitiated can go to become informed. Writing should be geared to the levels of the public. Although there may be information presented for the scholarly, there should be a preponderance that is designed and directed toward the general population.

Along with good writing, there needs to be good visual design. No matter how well written a text may be, if it is not presented well, it will not communicate efficiently. All of which is to say that text is not a secondary element in exhibition design. It is essential that textual materials be well designed and implemented with just as much attention applied to detail and quality as that afforded to the other design elements.

8

Computers in the exhibition environment

In the past, the management, planning, design, and production of exhibits has been accomplished by highly trained, experienced individuals with an arsenal of manual skills at their disposal. For many people investigating the field of museum exhibitions, the requisite capabilities have been outside their grasp. For many smaller institutions, especially those which preserve and exhibit local or regional heritage, the only way of obtaining professional, finished exhibitions has been to contract the task to others. While many fine firms are available to assist in the production of exhibitions, the reasonable expenses they require are often beyond the small institution's resources. Such museums are then left to do the best they can with what they have. Dedicated people who are striving to produce quality exhibits for their communities are always looking for ways to obtain the skills they need at affordable costs. Computers have been just the tool needed to accomplish many of the goals of such people.

In many ways the personal computer (PC) is *the* major new technological addition to the museum tool box. For the small and large institution, the computer has been a great boon. It enables administrators to plan and manage more effectively, and allows designers to quickly illustrate and develop ideas, build visual models, and test concepts. The accuracy and versatility of the computer coupled with other types of connected machines, called peripherals, has helped production staffs to generate text more easily, to create and execute professional-quality visual elements, and to make signage quickly when needed.

Product control and cost savings are two of the principal factors that affect production departments. Technology is sufficiently advanced now for publications and graphics in an exhibition to be produced in-house. Even if such materials are commercially produced, the control of production is largely in the hands of the designer. This saves greatly on time and production costs.

It is foreseeable that computer-aided manufacturing (CAM) systems will make production possible straight from the designer's mind to the completed product at a practical level. Computers can conserve not only time and materials, but also wear and tear on the production staff. While they are not, as yet, the exhibit builder's panacea that they may eventually become, there are currently some very practical and useful ways that computers can aid and enhance all aspects of museum exhibitions.

Even though the idea of purchasing a computer may seem too expensive or impractical for many small museums with limited resources, it should be noted that the cost of such equipment and the programs to operate it is becoming more reasonable all the time. What was completely unattainable five years ago is affordable now. The investment of money and time in acquiring computers, even to a limited extent, will often pay large dividends in terms of the capabilities available to a museum's staff. The real limitation is the willingness of the individuals to embark upon learning to use the new technology. It is highly probable that most museums will be "computerized" in some form before the turn of the century. Although some may use computers as nothing more than word processors for label production in the beginning, the seductive nature of the abilities afforded by automation and the ease with which they are acquired will eventually lead to wider and more expanded use.

This chapter is a look at some (not all) of the uses and capabilities computers make available now for exhibitors. It will offer some possibilities for the future as well. However, as with most predictions, the realities will no doubt far exceed the prognostications.

Computer capabilities and uses

People need and use information in many forms. The way information is stored and its ease of recovery are key factors in how useful it can be. Computers are machines designed to store and manage information in ways that are useful to people. It is important to understand what kinds of computer tools are available for managing information in order to make sensible choices about those that match needs with capabilities.

Computer programs have multitudinous formats, capabilities, and applications. The thousands of programs available are daunting to the newcomer and can pose a seemingly insurmountable barrier of intimidation. No one likes to feel incapable or deficient, and this desire to avoid embarrassment can prevent people from obtaining and using tools that will help them. Of the thousands of programs available, most are highly specialized to specific tasks and need not be considered in the more generalized museum application. The remaining types of programs might be broken down into three categories:

- word processors
- databases
- draw and paint programs

Word processors are used to create text documents such as letters, labels, newsletters, and other printed materials. Databases are programs that arrange and store pieces of information such as numbers, words, and pictures. The information is stored in groupings and can be manipulated in many useful ways. There are a variety of databases with particular capabilities. Draw and paint programs allow the computer to be used as a graphic tool. Pictures created in these programs can be used in a variety of ways such as to illustrate, to decorate and to record visual information.

Computers as exhibition elements

Computers have entered the interpretive milieu as well. In their simplest use, they can act passively as electronic labels and wayfinders. In more complex applications, they can serve as interactive tutors. One of the criteria for creating successful signage and labeling is that it should be attention-grabbing. The video display terminal, like other video devices such as televisions, has an intrinsic visual interest. When the elements of color and motion are added, the computer screen becomes a very attractive addition to the overall design in a gallery.

Another important aspect of the video image is that it has vast graphic range. The combination of graphic representation, verbal information, and interactive response stimulates participation and generates interest. "A picture is worth a thousand words" applies well to computer presentation. With its capability for animation, the computerized label can present very complex ideas in ways that are easier to understand. The viewer can learn relationships between systems such as energy transfer, food chains, or hydrology in a manner that appeals to both hemispheres of the brain. This cross-reinforcement leads to greater length of attention span and increased retention (see Chapter 2, pp. 30–1).

Although it has been available for a number of years, the computer as an exhibit device within the gallery has only now become technologically practical. Automated information systems are getting better and more fool-proof all the time. Interactive computer systems allow visitors to access information previously available only from a library and personal research, or as conveyed by lecturer or docent. These machines enhance visitor learning retention by interaction, while at the same time limiting handling of the mechanisms to the act of pointing. With present generations of children being trained in computer operation and usage, it is natural for them to expect the computer to be as much a part of the museum as it is in schools, home life, and business. Computer use in the exhibit context will increase and develop into a normal part of the exhibit developer's bag of tricks for getting the message across.

The development of input or "interface" devices such as touch screens has greatly reduced maintenance worries, while at the same time increasing audience participation. It is usually better to eliminate the keyboard as an option unless there is some essential function it serves. The "joy-stick" is still popular as a manipulative instrument, but they tend to break often. The "mouse" introduced a new way of manipulating the computer and created a user-friendly relationship between the visitor and the machine. The "trackball" mouse, a device that features an inset ball that controls the cursor's movement on the video screen, has offered ease of use as well as reduced the opportunity to damage the device. All of these options are available now as are a number of other forms of input devices. Experimentally, voice-activated and responsive input mechanisms are in use and will probably become the better solution for visitor participation.

At present, probably the best interactive device for manipulating the computer on exhibit is the touch screen. Safely sealing all other devices except the video screen itself from the user, the touch screen blends easy use with durability. Touch screens are increasingly popular in many of life's daily activities such as banking, wayfinding, and in education. Museums have several options available in touch screen technology. These include pre-packaged, ready-to-use programs for presentations that the museum staff is heavily involved in preparing.

The interaction between the visitor and the computer enhances an already important aspect of museum education. Self-paced learning has been one of the principal advantages of the museum educational environment. The computer allows even more control by the user. The possibility of providing information to the curious viewer is virtually limitless, yet the aspect of learning speed is still firmly in the user's control.

In terms of the visitor's capability to carry on his or her own research activities, the computer offers tremendous opportunities. Just as many libraries and archives are making records and research materials available via computer interfaces, museums are beginning to fashion similar banks of information.

The concept of a visitor being able to peruse collections (within limits, of course), access research documentation, and even examine images of collection items, expands the meaning and use of museums as educational and research institutions. It will be possible, for instance, for a patron, after viewing an exhibition on Native American pottery, to access additional information about the American Southwest, Native American symbolism, or New World ceramic technology. Even more broadly, he or she might search at leisure through ceramics of the world, the history and natural history of North America, or any number of other subject interests fostered by the exhibition.

In the Information Age, the role of museums will be expanded through changing technologies. The basic appeal of the actual object, the "real thing," will not diminish, but the intellectual curiosity engendered by exhibitions will find sustenance in information technology.

Computers in exhibition production

The computer has made a dramatic difference in the production end of exhibitions. There are many ways in which this is true. One of the first and simplest advantages to be realized from the new technology was in producing text and images. Software programs that allow a user to manipulate text are prolific. The typestyles available are numerous, with new ones being created and marketed every day. The human ability to read text places limits on how visually complex type may become and still be legible. However, available typestyles, sizes, and formats can be used to create textual imagery that is both eye-catching and pleasing. For textual "pictures" such as title signs and wayfinding devices, such creative capabilities strengthen the designer's options.

Beyond text is a whole realm of two-dimensional visual design. Creating logos, thematic images, and directional graphics is made easier and more exciting by using computer graphic programs. The accuracy of the images created on a computer screen is limited only by the kinds of devices used to print them. The costs for printing devices which are satisfactory for most exhibition purposes are becoming more and more reasonable. A standard resolution available with many laser printers is 300 dots per inch (dpi). This means that in each inch of the printing area, the printer is able to assemble as many as 300 dots of ink or toner. That degree of image resolution is normally quite adequate for graphic and text production. The need for higher resolution (more dots per inch) arises when the images are to be enlarged greatly. A 300 dpi image is usually satisfactory up to about a 300 percent increase in the size of the image. Beyond that, it may be better to transport the image on a disk to a commercial printing establishment with a machine capable of greater than 1200 dpi (see Chapter 7, p. 130).

Many museums cannot afford the high-end printing devices that refine images to 1200 dpi or more but most printing businesses have machines that can produce such resolutions. Indeed, many printing agencies have computers that are used to produce their own contracted jobs. The same machines are often able to accept a client's own disk from which to print his or her images. It is wise to explore local businesses' computer capabilities with a view to eventually using them as an output for in-house ideas.

In museums with silk screening shops, computer images are very useful. The ability of the machine to produce the image greatly reduces preparation time. Also, many graphics and text programs allow the image to be printed as a positive or a negative. In creating the stencils from which silk screens are produced, this is a tremendous advantage. This capability is also useful for producing text and graphic panels for back-lighting. Using a laser printer that can print on acetate, overhead projections panels, back-lit panels, and a variety of other applications are possible.

One of the premier ways that computer technology benefits museums is in its ability to visually display ideas. This can be done quickly on a computer screen with the added advantage that the images can be manipulated easily to create new arrangements. What can take hours and days to design and lay out on a drawing board using pens, rulers, T-squares, and X-acto knives, can now be produced in a fraction of that time. This capability helps to conserve two vital resources: time and money.

Layout and paste-up are functions that exhibit staffs have always had to face.

Layout programs enable the designer to assemble graphics from one program and text from another into one screen image. The parts can then be arranged and rearranged, sizes altered, and fonts selected to accomplish the design goals. The process of laying out and pasting up has been sped up immensely in the computer environment.

The greater speed at which images can now be rendered has reduced work-time costs and increased the number and scope of tasks that can be processed. Also, with the communications abilities already at hand, sharing and comparing of ideas in project groups is easier and more productive. In many ways, the new information technology can free designers to concentrate more on designing and less on producing "saleable" visual presentations.

Virtually all of the major computer manufacturers have hardware and software that allow the designer to present his or her concepts graphically. Computers can utilize a number of programs for every phase of design from scanning images or creating free-hand drawings, to producing three-dimensional images that take the viewer on a tour of the gallery. Text and graphics can be joined in a single document, generating camera-ready and finished artwork.

Using available programs and hardware, a whole realm of new possibilities opens up to the progressive designer. Programs to accomplish almost any task are available for most major brands of computers. Newer versions of programs are produced about once a year, and with each update greater potentials are realized. The next five to ten years will undoubtedly bring many new, exciting possibilities. Indeed, the computer as we now know it will probably be altered both in form and function far beyond what we can now imagine. However, it will be a while before the machines we use today are wholly obsolete, and in the meantime they are powerful production tools.

For the person who is not particularly interested or gifted in creating graphics, or is not familiar with using computers, there is a veritable profusion of clip-art and ready-made text formats available. Even if the ready-made art is not satisfactory, scanners can be used to capture images into the computer environment. A scanner is a machine that works similarly to a photocopy device. It "scans" an image like a photograph or drawing, line by line, then saves the image as digital information that the computer can use. Scanners open up a whole world of images. Care must be taken to avoid copyright violations, but for the most part, any image that can be photographed or drawn can be used by the computer. Some scanners can also record the colors of the images they capture. Using color computers and printers, many exciting designs are possible.

Computer-aided design (CAD) programs are now available for most computer types. These programs allow the designer to produce working drawings with measurements to scale. In some shops, CAD programs go directly from the computer screen to the blueprint. Corrections and modifications can be made and produced quickly. Production can proceed directly from the designer's ideas. This does have a caution attached, however. It calls for the designer to be more aware and competent in creating ideas that will work as presented. The computer, on the other hand, automatically provides many of the skills needed to render correct, usable architectural plans.

Some computers are specialized and intended for particular functions. Word processor machines are useful in text and label production but most do not have advanced graphic abilities. Other machines can produce vinyl lettering and cut-out materials. These are a form of CAM system. It is conceivable that in the near future CAM systems will play a major role in much of the physical production of exhibitions. The list of hardware and software is long and growing longer all the time, and with the refinements come increased capabilities for manipulating material objects.

The automobile manufacturing industry, along with many others, is heavily involved in CAM systems. Robots do much of the work today. These are CAM devices driven by computers. It is possible that similar tools will do much of the work in the exhibit workshop of the future.

Computers as administrative aids

One of the chief aids that the computer revolution has provided for exhibit administrators is the element of control. As an organizing and tracking medium, the computer, using appropriate software, is unsurpassed. Its ability to process information quickly provides a valuable managerial tool. Word processing is one of the elementary uses of the computer. The ability to set down words and then to review them before committing them to the printed form has reduced the amount of time and material needed to generate even a medium-size progress report, time sheet, or letter of agreement. As spell checking, lexicons, and style sheets are added, the word processing program is able to go beyond being a "super typewriter" and become a means of generating any form of printed material needed in exhibitry, from gallery notes to full-color catalogs. The advantage is that museum personnel can retain full control of the project from inception to production, thereby reducing delays, and avoiding endless proofreading and being at the mercy of the print shop's schedule.

Computers have provided another major capability in the form of large groupings of information called databases. Databases have been and are continually being built and expanded for purposes of collection, archival, and financial management. In some museums and libraries it is possible to do extensive research into the institutional holdings without disturbing the actual objects. This is particularly advantageous from a collection and archival management point of view, but it also impacts personnel time and facilities use as well. In addition, the capacity to explore new and uncharted associations in information has been greatly enhanced by the computer. Relationships never before conceived between objects, events, and records can be forged and expanded upon. As the museum community moves toward the day when databases are shared worldwide, the research attributes of the computer will continually grow and become increasingly in demand.

At a more practical and mundane level, using databases to keep track of objects, object information, money, materials, time, and personnel meets a fundamental exhibition development need: managing resources (see Chapter 1, p. 14). Very simple to operate, user-friendly programs can be effectual at this level. Normally the amount of information being managed is relatively small and the needs are straightforward, so there is no need for expensive and complex hardware or software. For instance, a flat database such as FileMaker Pro ™ (Claris) running on an Apple Macintosh computer can be used to record, sort, report, and track supply invoices, collection object movement, and scheduling matters. Similarly, for almost any type of personal computer there are programs already available at nominal prices for project-managing tasks. The documents are easy to create, require little in the way of disk storage space, and are flexible enough to be customized to the user's individualized needs. When their use is over, unless there is a need to archive the information, the documents can be deleted.

When considering a database there are two basic factors to keep in mind. What is the database for and what is it required to do? There are several different types of database programs: flat databases, relational databases, spreadsheet databases, and others that are hybrid programs. Databases are programs that contain a number of blocks of information called "fields." A field might contain the last name of each artist in the art collection, or the species name of specimens in a natural history collection. There are usually a number of fields for each object or item. They might include information like the accession and catalog numbers, the date of acceptance into the museum, the name of the donor, and the like. These fields are combined into one set of information about an object called a "record," and a compilation of records is called a "file." In most of the database programs, the user can specify which fields are desired, either by creating and customizing the fields themselves, or by telling the software supplier what he or she wants. In addition, the look of the records, the way they are printed, and other visual aspects can be determined by the user.

A flat database is a compilation of records in which every record contains the same number of fields, whether there is information in them or not. Flat databases are very useful for setting up groups of information quickly that have a great deal of shared or similar information. For instance, each record in an address list or set of exhibition labels contains about the same amount and type of data. Since most of the fields are used for each record, the flat database works quite well with little waste of electronic storage space. In a flat database, whether a field is filled or not, it still takes up the same amount of memory and storage space. In databases where the fields are empty for many of the records, machine and disk memory is wasted in storing nothing. In instances such as multi-collection records, there is a wide variety of information for the objects, often of differing kinds. For this sort of information the relational database may serve better.

Relational databases are groupings of small databases that are linked or "related" by a common element. The small flat databases are often called "tables." Each table contains fields that are useful for the particular kind of records in it. Information such as the institutional identification, accession numbers, and registration information for all collections might be contained in one table. For groups of information that are more specific to the types of collection, other tables are needed. For example, the data about historical furniture differ greatly from those for scientific bird specimens. Two different tables would be required to handle such diverse information. In that way, space is not wasted on empty fields.

Each small database or table has one field that is the same as all other tables within a larger database. This allows the tables to be "linked" by a common thread. In many museums, the accession or registration number is used as the linking item. Tables contain object provenance, research documentation, conservation history, and a number of other kinds of information. The relational computer program allows the user to establish links, gather, and arrange information from all the tables into a set of data about an object or groups of objects. An example might be to find all the objects and specimens in a museum that were collected by a certain person, or donated by a particular benefactor, or that represent a specific span of time. The possibilities for gathering and arranging information are virtually endless.

Establishing relational databases is complex and time-consuming. It is usually best left to an expert to create and maintain such systems. There are a few relational database programs commercially available for museums, most of which are targeted for collection management or fund-raising. The advantages of the relational databases over flat ones are the economy of memory required and the speed at which a relational database can search out information when dealing with records numbering in the thousands or even millions.

Spreadsheet database programs are targeted toward numerical records such as budgetary information. They are useful in financial management and come with a variety of services. They can compute numerical records, draw graphs and charts representing the data contained, and create reports that are useful in keeping track of information.

In looking for the right program, it is useful to set down in writing what is needed and desired, and then decide which of the available programs meets those needs best. It is a good idea to consult with someone familiar with these kinds of programs. A person in computer hardware and software sales can often help. At times, especially when considering something as complex as a relational database, a paid consultant is a wise investment. It is best to seek someone without commercial interest in the specific programs under consideration. The need is to get what will work best, not necessarily what a person is selling.

Conclusions

The idea of automating the exhibition process is taking shape. Many institutions have already taken the first steps in the process. Others have adopted a wait-and-see attitude. There is a basic distrust of machines on the part of many. Intimidation and fear play roles in keeping some exhibitors from actively participating in the computer revolution.

Many universities, colleges, and continuing education programs offer short courses in computer usage and training in specific software for newcomers. These can take the newcomer from computer illiteracy all the way to expertise. The perception that only programmers can master the use of computers is incorrect. One does not have to understand the internal combustion engine to drive a car. We do not have to be able to disassemble and rebuild a watch or calculator to use them. There are many individuals who are busily creating programs for users to operate. Unless one is interested in programming, there is no need to address the issue at all to use a computer quite satisfactorily.

For some people there may exist a feeling that they will somehow be replaced by the machine and their usefulness as creators ended. This is one of the basic areas of resistance to using computers. However, until a machine is built that can think, humans must give the orders, and in endeavors that require ingenuity, intuition, and inspiration, computers will never replace people.

Another perception acts as a deterrent for some – that computers are still evolving and therefore it is wise to wait until they stabilize before investing. This is akin to avoiding the telephone until the cellular phone was invented. The technology will continue to grow and develop. There will never be a time when hardware and software will become static and uniform. There is no time like the present to jump in and learn to swim. The sooner one becomes computer literate and competent, the sooner one will stop being bewildered by the rapidity of change, and feeling left out and left behind.

Even if the idea of computers in the design studio seems abhorrent or intimidating, it is the way of the future. It is clearly advisable, probably essential, that exhibit designers make the relatively easy transition from pencil-and-paper technology to one that enhances their own natural genius and productivity. To maintain an outdated *status quo* by resisting a move into the future illustrates what Ralph Waldo Emerson penned, "A foolish consistency is the hobgoblin of little minds."

Appendix 1

Infestation report

Infestation Report	**MUSEUM OF MAN IN THE NEW WORLD** **CITY, STATE 79406-3191**

1. Date of Report: _____

2. Date Infestation Detected: _____ SAMPLE FORM

3. Person Investigating: _____

4. Collection/Division involved: _____

5. Specific Location of Infestation: _____

6. Identification of Infesting Organism: _____

    Life stage(s): _____

    Measurements: _____

7. Target Material: _____

8. Description of Infestation: _____

9. Action(s) taken: _____

10. Chemical/Physical agent(s) used: _____

    Repellant: _____

    Fumigant: _____

    Freeze Chamber: ☐   Temp: _____ Duration: _____

11. Recommended follow-up procedures:

    1) _____

    2) _____

    3) _____

Report filed by: _____ Date: _____

Copies to: Director   Assistant Director   Registrar   Curator(s) of Collections

145

Appendix 2

Exhibition request form

Exhibition Request Form

Send, mail, or FAX the completed form to:

Museum Address
City, State or Province ZIP Code
(A/C) Telephone #
FAX #

For Administrative Use :
Exhibit Request Number _____
Date received _____
Date reviewed _____
Approved? ☐ YES   ☐ NO

Requestor Information

Requestor(s): _____

Division(s): _____ Telephone: _____

General Information

Subject or Title of Proposed Exhibition: _____
_____

Proposed exhibit duration

☐ 6–8 weeks ....Short Term

☐ 12 weeks–1 year ....Temporary

☐ 1–3 years ....Long Term

Proposed beginning date

_____	_____	_____
(day)	(month)	(year)

Proposed ending date

_____	_____	_____
(day)	(month)	(year)

What gallery space is preferred? _____
_____
_____

Provide at least one of the following measurements, if possible:

　　Approximate number of **Linear Feet** required　_____

　　Approximate number of **Square Feet** required　_____

Object Information

Give an approximate number and/or descriptions of objects/artifacts proposed to be included in the exhibition

_____

_____

_____

_____

Is the exhibition to be loaned from another institution or traveling exhibition service

☐ Yes ☐ No

If Yes, list the source(s): _____

_____

Is the exhibition to be produced from within the Museum's collections (In-house)?.......... ☐ Yes ☐ No

If Yes, from which collection(s)/division(s)? _____

Will the exhibition include objects/artifacts from lending institution(s)? .... ☐ Yes ☐ No

If Yes, list the institution(s): _____

If the exhibition is produced In-house, is it to travel from the Museum? .... ☐ Yes ☐ No

If Yes, outline the proposal: _____

Justification

Briefly stated, why do you feel the Museum should present the proposed exhibition? _____

_____

_____

_____

_____

_____

_____

_____

_____

_____

(Attach additional pages as needed)

Publications and Programs

Is a catalog proposed for the exhibition?.. ☐ Yes ☐ No

If Yes, provide the following information:

Approx. number of pages _____ and overall dimensions_____

              Color photos?........................... ☐ Yes ☐ No

              Black/White photos?.............. ☐ Yes ☐ No

              Other graphics?....................... ☐ Yes ☐ No   Describe _____

Are other publications planned such as gallery guides, posters, or brochures? .... ☐ Yes ☐ No

If Yes, what do you foresee?   _____

_____

What programs or special events are proposed to enhance or accompany the exhibition?

            Opening reception .... ☐ Yes ☐ No

            Lecture series .... ☐ Yes ☐ No

            Films.. ☐ Yes ☐ No

            Workshop(s)... ☐ Yes ☐ No

            Seminar(s)... ☐ Yes ☐ No

            Outreach programs.. ☐ Yes ☐ No

            Gallery talk(s) .... ☐ Yes ☐ No

            Other (please specify):   _____

What audience or audiences do you think the exhibition will attract?

_____

_____

_____

_____

Are speakers, demonstrators, teachers, etc. to participate?.. ☐ Yes ☐ No

If Yes, list their name(s), title(s), and affiliation(s):

_____

_____

_____

_____

_____

_____

(attach additional pages as needed)

Projected Budget Information (Optional)

Provide an <u>ESTIMATED BUDGET</u> for the proposed exhibition using the specified categories   (attach additional pages as needed)

A) PRODUCTION (Supplies and materials needed to produce the exhibition)

Items	Amount

Total...........

B.) PUBLICATIONS (Printed material to enhance, publicize and document the exhibit)

Items	Amount

Total...........

C) SHIPPING (List name of carrier and distance from port to port upon which the estimate is based)

Items	Amount

Total...........

D) FEES (Rental costs, consultant's, writer's, or speaker's fees and/or honoraria)

Items	Amount

Total...........

E) INSURANCE (Include an approximate dollar valuation of the object/artifacts as a basis for the estimate)

Items	Amount

Total...........

F) OTHER (<u>Specify items</u>. Include estimates for receptions, workshops, additional educational materials, conservation, etc.)

Items	Amount

Total...........

GRAND TOTAL--$

Appendix 3

Checklist for exhibition development

Checklist For Exhibition Development

Date _____   Exhibit Request Number _____

Title of Exhibit _____

√	Activity	Decision	Date

Section A - For exhibits circulated by individuals or traveling exhibition services

☐ Director's decision to approve....................................... ☐ YES ☐ No _____

    If **YES**, the exhibition is scheduled for_____19_____

                    through_____19_____

    In gallery(ies) _____

    If **NO**, has a

☐ Rejection letter been sent to Requestor........................... ☐ YES ☐ No_____

Section B - Director's delegation for exhibition planning

Project Director/Manager   _____

Curator(s)/Subject Expert   _____

Registrar   _____

Designer   _____

Educator   _____

Section C - Budget development

☐ Budget proposal submitted? Date _____

POSSIBLE FUNDING SOURCES IDENTIFIED

√	Type	Source	Amount	Y/N
☐	Private sources	1)_____		☐
	(Individuals, trusts, small	2)_____		☐
	businesses, etc.)	3)_____		☐
☐	Support organizations	1) _____		☐
		2)_____		☐
		3)_____		☐
☐	Museum funding	1)_____		☐
	(Accounts, divisions, etc.)	2)_____		☐
		3)_____		☐
☐	Other sources	1)_____		☐
	(Corporations, endowments,	2)_____		☐
	etc.)	3)_____		☐

155

Section D- Exhibition Budget

☐ Budget established and approved_____

  1) Production cost ...._____

  2) Publications (Catalogs, Gallery Guides, etc.) ...._____

  3) Shipping charges..._____

  4) Fees..._____

  5) Insurance..._____

  6) Other ...._____

     ...._____

  Final Total ...._____

Date final budget approved   _____

Additional budgetary notes

Section E - Timeline

date	Requirement or Activity	Date Completed	Assignment To
_____ ☐	Timeline completed	_____	Planners
_____ ☐	Preliminary script completed	_____	Curator
_____ ☐	Object/artifact list finalized	_____	Curator
_____ ☐	Gallery/production plans due	_____	Designer
_____ ☐	Exhibit supplies ordered	_____	Designer
_____ ☐	Exhibit supplies received	_____	Designer
_____ ☐	Publicity plan formulated	_____	As Assigned
_____ ☐	Publications text/graphics due	_____	Curator
_____ ☐	Publications review completed	_____	Curator
_____ ☐	Publications items sent to printer	_____	Curator
_____ ☐	Educational plans completed	_____	Educator
_____ ☐	Exhibit label/text to Exhibits Div.	_____	Curator
_____ ☐	Exhibit graphics to Exhibits Div.	_____	Curator
_____ ☐	Shipping arrangements finalized	_____	Registrar
_____ ☐	Insurance arrangements finalized	_____	Registrar
_____ ☐	Objects/artifacts delivered	_____	Curator
_____ ☐	Condition report completed	_____	Registrar/Curator
_____ ☐	Publ. received and approved	_____	Curator
_____ ☐	Educational materials completed	_____	Educator

157

_____ ☐	Docent training completed	_____	Educator
_____ ☐	Reception plannned/approved	_____	Team
_____ ☐	Space and services confirmed	_____	Team
_____ ☐	Exhibit installation completed	_____	Designer
_____ ☐	Director's walk-through	_____	Designer/Curator
_____ ☐	Security walk-through	_____	Designer/Curator

Exhibition OPENING DATE:

- Preview opening?   ☐ **YES** ☐ No If Yes, date, time, and place _____

- Media coverage?   ☐ **YES** ☐ No If Yes, date, time, and place _____
  Museum contact person _____

- Is a reception or special event planned?   ☐ **YES** ☐ **NO**   If Yes, give

  Date_____ Time from _____ to _____

  Location _____ Hosting group(s)_____

Exhibition CLOSING DATE:

Date	√	Task	Personnel	Team Mmbrs
_____	☐	Dismantling completed	_____	Designer/Curator
_____	☐	Packing for shipment completed	_____	Curator/Registrar
_____	☐	Shipping completed	_____	Registrar
_____	☐	Budget/accounting report rec'd	_____	As Assigned
_____	☐	Evaluative report compiled	_____	Whole Team

(For other special requirements, attach additional pages)

Glossary

Terminology is one of the areas in communication where people often encounter difficulties. The glossary presented here is not meant as an absolute definition of the terms included, rather it is to help the reader understand what the author is intending to say.

accession the process of transferring title or ownership from the providing source (field work, purchase, gift, transfer, etc.) to the museum

acid-free a term generally referring to either paper or paper-board that has been treated (buffered) or made from fibers free of organic acids

acquisition the act of gaining physical possession of an object, specimen, or sample

acrylic paint a term referring to a number of plastic, water-based paint products

affective learning learning based upon emotional response to stimuli; emotional learning

angle iron a metal construction material with a cross-section in the form of the letter "L"

anodized metal a metal which has been coated with another material through the process of electrolysis

application software that allows the computer to perform specific tasks; software program

appraisal the assigning of a monetary value to an object

architect's rule or scale a graduated device used to make scaled measurements

artifact an object, either two- or three-dimensional, that has been selected, altered, used, or made by human effort

audience all or a specially identified segment of a museum constituency

audiovisual devices machines that produce sound and images

blockbuster a term derived from the popular name of the huge German bombs used in World War II to blast large sections of a city; in the museum sense, it refers to a revolutionary, powerful exhibition

board foot a USA standard length measurement of sawn wood by which the purchase price is figured

box-in-a-box configuration a frame of reference that views micro-environments as existing in and dependent upon their surrounding macro-environments

buffer a material or condition interposed between two other materials or conditions to reduce or slow the interaction between them

CAD (computer-aided design system): a hardware + software system that allows the operator to accomplish design and layout tasks on a computer

case furniture structures used within cases, vitrines, or on bases that serve as supporting surfaces for objects/graphics

cataloging assigning an object to an established classification system and initiating a record of the nomenclature, provenance, number, and location of that object in the collection storage area

ceiling grid generally refers to the metal support structure for drop ceilings

central processing unit see "CPU"

coating paint, stain, or plaster used to finish a surface

159

cognitive learning knowledge based upon reasoned thought; rational learning

collection an identifiable selection of objects having some significant commonality

collection manager a person charged with the care of a particular collection, normally working under the direction of a curator

collective medium a particular means of expression used by more than one person in a collective effort, and for predetermined and agreed upon goals

comfort freedom from stress or the fear of failure

communication "the transfer of information and ideas with the deliberate intention to achieve certain changes, deemed desirable by the sender, in the knowledge, opinions, attitudes and/or behavior of the receiver [sic]"[1]

composite board any material made of wood chips or sawdust bonded into sheets with adhesives; this includes materials such as particle board, chip board, and masonite

computer-aided design system see "CAD"

computer program see "application"

computer system the internal software that directs the computer's primary operations such as opening applications, finding stored data, and similar functional requirements

concept-oriented exhibition a presentation that is focused upon the transmission of information and in which collection objects may or may not be used to support the story rather than being the main emphasis

conflict of interest those acts or activities that may be construed to be contrary to ethical museum practices based on knowledge, experience, and contracts gained through conditions of employment

conservation the processes of preserving and protecting objects from loss, decay, damage, or other forms of deterioration

conservator a person with the appropriate scientific training to examine museum objects, work to prevent their deterioration, and provide the necessary treatment and repairs

controlled environment surroundings in which temperature, relative humidity, direct sunlight, pollution, and other atmospheric conditions are regulated

coordinating activities efforts aimed at keeping every task moving toward the same goal

copy written material from which text, labels, titles, sub-titles, etc. may be derived

cove base material used along the base of a wall

CPU (central processing unit): the machine that contains the processors and other circuitry and acts as the "brain" of a computer

cultural heritage a tradition, habit, skill, art form, or institution that is passed from one generation to the next.

cultural property the material manifestation of the concepts, habits, skills, art, or institutions of a specific people in a defined period of time

curator a museum staff member or consultant who is a specialist in a particular field of study and who provides information, does research, and oversees the maintenance, use, and enhancement of collections

cursor an image on the computer monitor that indicates the location for information input or activity

deaccession the process of removing objects from a museum's collections

deed of gift a document with the signature of the donor transferring title of an object to a museum

designer a museum staff member or consultant who designs the exhibition, does working drawings, and coordinates fabrication and installation activities

director the person providing conceptual leadership of the museum and charged with the responsibility for policy-making, funding, planning, organizing, staffing, supervising, and coordinating activities through the staff; the director is also responsible for the professional practices of the museum

display a presentation of objects for public view without significant interpretation added, relying solely upon the intrinsic merit of that which is presented. In the UK and Europe this word is used by choice instead of exhibition (q.v.)

distributed materials printed pamphlets, booklets, catalogs, gallery notes, and other materials that are distributed as part of the presentation of an exhibition

drive a device that receives and operates a disk for the computer's use

dry mount a method of bonding two surfaces together using heat-sensitive tissue and a heating instrument; normally used for mounting two-dimensional objects such as photographs or drawings

drywall see "sheetrock"

drywall screw a specialized screw used for attaching sheetrock to the studs

educator a museum staff person or consultant who specializes in museum education and who produces instructional materials, advises about educational content for exhibitions, and oversees the implementation of educational programs

electrical the term for any construction elements concerned with supplying or controlling electricity

endowment a funding process in which a stated part of a money gift (corpus) is held to generate income and only that income may be spent

ethics the process of establishing principles of right behavior that may serve as action guides for individuals or groups

ethnic used in the museum community as a non-discriminatory term referring to a division or group of people distinguishable by language, custom, or some special characteristic

evaluation report a document that sets down evaluation findings assessing an exhibition from the standpoints of meeting goals and successful development

exhibit (noun) a grouping of objects and interpretive materials that form a unit for presentation; the localized grouping of objects and interpretive materials that form a cohesive unit within a gallery

exhibit (verb) to present or expose to view, show, or display

exhibit case a closed, internally lit piece of exhibit furniture within which objects and/or graphics are exhibited

exhibit panel a vertical surface upon which objects/graphics or support devices are attached for exhibit purposes, or for use as a spatial divider

exhibition (noun) a comprehensive grouping of all the elements (including exhibits and displays) that form a complete public presentation of collections and information for the public use; "An exhibition is a means of communication aiming at large groups of the public with the purpose of conveying information, ideas, and emotions relating to the material evidence of man and his surrounding, with the aid of chiefly visual and dimensional methods"[2]

exhibition (verb) the act or fact of exhibiting collections, objects, or information to the public for the purpose of education, enlightenment, and enjoyment

exhibition policy a written document that states a museum's philosophy and intent toward public exhibitions

expansion joint a joint between structural elements which employs a flexible separator that allows expansion and contraction of materials to occur without damage

extermination the acts of either preventing the invasion of harmful organisms or ridding a collection or collection items of an existing infestation through the use of chemical or mechanical means not considered dangerous to humans in the dosages needed to kill the pests

fabrication the work of creating the physical elements needed for the presentation of collection objects in an exhibition; the process of constructing props, preparing graphics, building cases, etc.

facility the physical components that comprise the buildings and grounds of an institution; the physical plant

fire rating a rating system developed to indicate the relative resistance a material has to burning through and its ability to prevent the spread of fire; usually measured in time units

floppy disk a portable, plastic disk coated with a material sensitive to magnetic fields that can be used to store information generated by a computer

fluorescent lighting light sources in which electric current is passed through gases in a glass tube causing them to fluoresce and produce illumination

footcandle a unit for measuring illumination equal to the amount of light reaching a surface 1 ft sq. produced by a candle 1 ft away

Formica[R] a brand name that has become the generic term for numerous types of commercially produced, high-density plastic laminates

framing the method of creating a stable opening into which a window or doorway can be built

fumigation the use of a highly toxic chemical gas to kill any organisms existing in the target area or item; the chemicals utilized in fumigation are highly dangerous to humans and their use is controlled by law

161

furring the method of covering an I-beam or other construction element with another material to disguise it

gallery a room specifically designated for exhibitions

gallery guides a form of distributed material; written documents, usually brief and easy to carry, that are available for visitors to have and use to gain more information about an exhibition subject

"Gee Whiz!" factor the tendency of humans to react strongly, positively or in awe toward something presented that is large, colorful, famous, or in some other way out of the ordinary — hence the reaction, "Gee Whiz!" or "Oh! Wow!"

graphic a two-dimensional depiction such as a photograph, painted design, drawing, silkscreen, etc. used to impart information, draw attention, or illustrate

grout material used to fill spaces between ceramic tiles

hard copy a printed document from a computer

hard disk a computer device that is more durable and stable, usually contains more memory space, and possesses greater speed than a floppy disk

hardware electronic machinery; used to refer to a computer and its peripheral machines such as printers, plotters, monitors, etc.

hardwood any wood from deciduous trees usually having a rather fine grain and resistance to chipping and splintering. Often used for framing and finishing surfaces

historic site a location with important historic connections usually relating to an important person or event

HVAC heating, ventilation, and air conditioning system

hydrated salts chemicals that are hydrophilic and can be used to control relative humidity in enclosed spaces; among these are sodium chloride, zinc sulfate, magnesium nitrate, magnesium chloride, and lithium chloride

hydrophilic substances materials that readily absorb atmospheric water and are used as humidity buffers

I-beam a steel beam with a cross-section that is the shape of the letter "I"

ICCROM (International Center for the Study of the Preservation and the Restoration of Cultural Property): an intergovernmental organization created by UNESCO in 1969, whose statutory functions are to collect and disseminate documentation of scientific problems of conservation; to promote research in this field; to provide advice on technical questions; and to assist in training technicians and raising the standard of restoration work. Address: Via di San Michele, 13, 00153 Rome, Italy

ICOM (International Council of Museums): the international non-governmental organization of museum and professional museum workers established to advance the interests of museology and other disciplines concerned with museum management and operations. Address: Maison de l'Unesco, 1 rue Miollis, 75732 Paris Cedex 15, France[3]

ICOM *Statutes* adopted by the 16th General Assembly of ICOM in The Hague, 5 September, 1989, the ICOM *Statutes* describe and define the ICOM organization, its role, membership, method, and objectives

ICTOP (International Committee for Training of Personnel): one of the standing committees of ICOM

incandescent lighting light sources in which an electric current causes a filament to glow or incandesce, producing illumination

inert products made of non-reactive, chemically balanced materials with special attention given to acidic neutrality

infestation a population of living organisms that exists in collections or collection items; the organisms may be as large as rats and mice, or as small as moths or fungi

infrared radiation (IR): the part of the electromagnetic spectrum below visible light that humans interpret as heat

input information or data that is typed, scanned, or otherwise digitized into the memory of a computer

interactive a device that invites and accommodates interaction between the viewer and itself

International Center for the Study of the Preservation and the Restoration of Cultural Property see "ICCROM"

International Committee for Training and Personnel see "ICTOP"

International Council of Museums see "ICOM"

interpretation the act or process of explaining or clarifying, translating, or presenting a personal understanding about a subject or object

inventory an itemized list of the objects included in a museum's collections

IR see "infrared radiation"

keyboard the device that allows a person to input data and direct the activities of the computer

label a textual graphic that provides information

latex paint a term referring to a number of plastic, water-based paint products

lathe thin strips of material, generally wood, used to form a matrix over which some other material may be applied; for example, lathe might be used between a concrete wall and plywood panels, or a lathe matrix might be used on a ceiling before plaster is applied

layout a composition using graphic design elements placed in relation to each other

left brain the left hemisphere of the human brain; the center for analytical thought, language, reasoning, reading, writing, and counting

leisure activities activities that people engage in when they are not involved in a professional pursuit

lux a unit of illumination equal to the illumination of a 1 m sq. surface uniformly 1 m away from a candle; equal to 5 footcandles

macro-environments the totality of the surrounding conditions and circumstances present in spaces generally room-size and larger

management-oriented activities tasks that focus on providing the resources and personnel needed to realize a product

Maslow's Hierarchy a behavioral construction by Abraham H. Maslow that relates the sequential and consecutive nature of human needs to motivations[4]

masonry refers to construction elements formed of brick, concrete blocks, or other similar materials

mechanical a term referring to any construction elements concerned with HVAC

micro-environments the totality of the surrounding conditions and circumstances present in small, often enclosed spaces

mildew microscopic fungi that attack organic materials that are exposed to high humidity and dampness

mission statement a written document that states a museum's institutional philosophy, scope, and responsibility

model a three-dimensional representation of an object or space usually using scaled measurements

monitor a video device on which the computer displays information

mounting the attachment of an object/graphic to a supporting surface; the device used to attach an object

mouse an input device that moves a cursor on the computer monitor and activates various functions of the computer

mud thinned plaster used to fill cracks and seams in a plaster or drywall surface

museology the branch of knowledge concerned with the study of the theories, procedures, concepts, and organization of museums

museum a non-profit-making, permanent institution that is in the service of society and is open to the public; it acquires, conserves, researches, communicates, and exhibits, for purposes of study, education and enjoyment, material evidence of people and their environment[5]

natural buffering the interaction between collection objects and their surroundings in an enclosed space that reduces or slows fluctuations in relative humidity and temperature

natural light the light produced by the sun that penetrates the Earth's atmosphere

nomenclature a system of names used to describe museum objects

object file a careful listing of all actions or activities impacting a particular object in the museum's collections including all conservation, restoration, exhibition, loan, or other uses of the object

object-oriented exhibition a presentation of collection objects with a primary goal of providing their exposure to public view with limited interpretation

open storage the practice of placing stored collections on public view without interpretation or planned educational content

particulate matter any materials capable of being airborne; dust

patrimony cultural property, both intellectual and real, passed from one generation to the next

pattern recognition a visual–mental process that seeks and recognizes familiar things or patterns

pH-balanced a neutral balance of acid and alkaline

plate the horizontal structural members in a wall (i.e., floor plate, header or top plate) to which the vertical members are attached

plenum the space above ceilings between floors or roofs

Plexiglasᴿ a brand name for formed, solid acrylic that has become a generic term used to refer to many commercially produced products; clear sheet acrylic is often used as a substitute for glass

plywood a building material made of thin sheets of sawn wood, laminated with adhesives to form larger sheets

pollutants gases and airborne particulate matter usually resulting from combustion or venting of chemicals associated with human, industrial, or other activities

polyvinyl acetate see "PVA"

preparation arranging, attaching, supporting, and other such activities that prepare an object/graphic for exhibit

presentation an oral communication of ideas using textual, graphic, and/or three-dimensional representations as aids to understanding; specifically for exhibits, the presentation of the design to the client for their consideration

preventive conservation collection care to minimize conditions that may cause damage

printer a mechanical device that receives information from a computer and prints it on to a tangible surface

product-oriented activities exhibition development efforts concerned with collection objects and interpretive aims

production the combined activities of fabrication, preparation, facilities renovation, and installation of exhibitions

project manager a staff person who oversees the whole process of exhibition development by facilitating communication and assisting in providing resources, with the goal of seeing the project through to its predetermined objectives

props exhibit properties; those items such as case furniture, exhibit cases, vitrines, panels, etc. that serve as the environmental elements for the presentation of the exhibits

psychrometer a device for measuring relative humidity using the differences in the measurements from dry- and wet-bulb thermometers in moving air

PVA (polyvinyl acetate): a thermoplastic with good aging characteristics sometimes used as a fixative or sealing agent

100 percent rag a term referring to the material content of paper or board indicating a fiber composition other than wood – usually cotton or linen

RAM (random access memory): the amount of memory indigenous to the computer with which it carries out its functions

random access memory see "RAM"

read only memory see "ROM"

recording hygrothermograph a device for measuring and recording on a paper chart both temperature and humidity over time

registrar the person charged with registering objects accessioned into a museum's collections, maintaining the registration records, and assigning the accession number

registration assigning a permanent number to an object entering a museum's collections for the purpose of identification and collection management

relative humidity see "RH"

relic a non-specific term used to describe things from the past, sometimes applied to ethnographic or historic objects

RH (relative humidity): the amount of water in a given volume of air compared to the amount of water vapor the same volume of air will hold at saturation (100 per cent RH) at a given temperature

right brain the right hemisphere of the human brain; the center for intuitive thought, emotional or affective learning, and visualization

ROM (read only memory): memory that the computer uses to store information and from which it draws data into the RAM to carry out specific functions

scale a system of measurement ratios in which real world data are converted to fractional equivalents while retaining proportional relationships

scaled drawing a graphic representation using scaled measurements

scanner an electronic device that "reads" images from documents and transforms them into digital information that the computer can manipulate

sheetrock a construction material made of gypsum powder bonded with an adhesive and sandwiched between layers of paper; also known as gypboard or drywall

silica gel a commonly used hydrophilic substance composed of a silicon + oxygen bond, neutral toward other substances, that can be used to control relative humidity within closed containers

software application, computer program; programmed information which instructs the computer as to its tasks

softwood any wood from an evergreen such as pine, fir, hemlock or cypress

specimen an example of a particular class of objects normally used when referring to natural science collections

strategic planning sometimes called forward or long-range planning – the process integrates the physical, educational, fiscal, and personnel goals of the museum or a particular collection area

stud a primary construction member of either wood or metal

stud wall a wall construction method using vertical and horizontal members (wood or metal) over which a "skin" of paneling is applied

study collection objects collected and organized for research or instructional use rather than for exhibition

sub-title an intermediate level of written information graphic, usually larger in typesize than a text block, and used to differentiate or emphasize sub-groupings within an exhibition

tactile exhibits exhibits that are designed to be touched

tamper-proof requiring a specialized instrument to operate

target audience any sub-group within a population that can be identified by some common factor or factors, and that is specifically chosen as a group to be attracted

text or text block a written graphic that aids in the interpretation of groups of objects or exhibition sections

thematic exhibitions exhibitions based upon a connecting theme that directs the choice of collection objects and information content

thermohygrometer a device for measuring temperature and humidity levels

tiles finishing elements made from a variety of different materials and usually held in place with an adhesive; ceramic, vinyl, and acoustic are a few of the materials used

title sign a graphic, often combining both text and pictorial design elements, usually placed at the entry to a gallery to attract attention and to announce the title of the exhibition

traffic flow refers to the movement of people through a specified area, usually a gallery

two-by-four a USA standard for pre-cut wood which actually measures about 1¾ in. (4.45 cm) by 3¾ in. (9.52 cm)

UBC (universal building code): a standardized set of specifications used as requirements for materials and the design of buildings in the USA

ultraviolet light see "UV light"

UNESCO United Nations Educational, Scientific, and Cultural Organization

UNESCO Convention this Convention on the Means of Prohibiting and Preventing the Illicit Import, Export, and Transfer of Ownership of Cultural Property aims to provide a process among nations for regulating international trade in cultural property

universal building code see "UBC"

UV light (ultraviolet light): the part of the electromagnetic spectrum immediately above the visible range; black light

VALS (Values and Lifestyles Segments): a generalized socio-economic structure by Arnold Mitchell that helps identify population segments, interests, and motivations by their collective values and lifestyles[6]

Values and Lifestyles Segments see "VALS"

vinyl adhesive glue used to adhere wallpapers and vinyl wall coverings to surfaces

visible light spectrum see "VLS"

vitrine a closed, externally lit piece of exhibit furniture, typically consisting of a base or pedestal with a clear enclosure for displaying objects/ graphics

165

VLS (visible light spectrum): those frequencies of the electromagnetic spectrum to which the human eye is visually sensitive; radiation that is perceived as light

wayfinder any visual, tactile, or auditory clues or devices that assist visitors in orienting themselves within a museum's facilities and surroundings, inform the audience of their options, and help them locate destinations

wet mount the process of attaching a photograph or other flat object to a surface using water-based adhesives

world view an individual's rational model of reality; one's mental picture of the world consisting of facts, raw perceptual data, concepts, suppositions, theories, and generalizations

Notes

Introduction

1 Loomis, Ross J. (1987) *Museum Visitor Evaluation: New Tool for Management*, Nashville, TN: American Association for State and Local History, p. 160.
2 Vehaar, Jan and Han Meeter (1989) *Project Model Exhibitions*, Holland: Reinwardt Academie, p. 28.

1 The exhibition development process

1 Vehaar, Jan and Han Meeter (1989) *Project Model Exhibitions*, Holland: Reinwardt Academie, p. 4.

2 Audiences and learning

1 Mitchell, Arnold (1983) *The Nine American Lifestyles*, New York: Warner Books.
2 Maslow, Abraham H. (1954) *Motivation and Personality*, New York: Harper & Row.
3 Hood, Marilyn G. (1983) "Staying Away: Why People Choose Not to Visit Museums," *Museum News* 61, 4 (April): pp. 50–7.
4 Conroy, Pete (1988) "Chapter 20: Cheap Thrills and Quality Learning," in Steve Bitgood (ed.) *Visitor Studies – 1988*, Jacksonville, AL: Center for Social Design, p. 189.

3 Designing exhibitions

1 Loomis, Ross J. (1987) *Museum Visitor Evaluation: New Tool for Management*, Nashville, TN: American Association for State and Local History, p. 161.

4 Controlling the exhibition environment

1 Stolow, Nathan (1977) "The Microclimate: A Localized Solution," Washington, DC: American Association of Museums, p. 1.

6 Exhibition evaluation

1 Loomis, Ross J. (1987) *Museum Visitor Evaluation: New Tool for Management*, Nashville, TN: American Association for State and Local History, p. 202.
2 ibid., p. 203.
3 Screven, C. G. (1977) "Some Thoughts on Evaluation," *The Visitor and the Museum*, Washington, DC: American Association of Museums, p. 31.
4 Loomis, op cit., p. 202.
5 Loomis, op cit., p. 202.
6 Screven, C. G. (1976) "Exhibit Evaluation: A Goal-Referenced Approach," *Curator* 19, 4 (December): pp. 271–90.
7 Barker, R. G. (1963) *The Stream of Behavior*, New York: Appleton-Century-Crofts; Barker, R. G. (1965) "Explorations in Ecological Psychology," *American Psychologist* 20: pp. 1–14.
8 Wolf, Robert L. (1980) "A Naturalistic View of Evaluation," *Museum News* 58, 1 (September): pp. 39–45.
9 Wolf, Robert L. and Barbara L. Tymitz (1979) *A Preliminary Guide for Conducting Naturalistic Evaluation in Studying Museum Environments*, Washington, DC: Office of Museum Programs, Smithsonian Institution, pp. 5–9.
10 Hood, Marilyn G. (1983) "Staying Away: Why People Choose Not to Visit Museums," *Museum News* 61, 4 (April): pp. 50–7.

11 Alt, M. B. and K. M. Shaw, (1984) "Characteristics of Ideal Museum Exhibits," *British Journal of Psychology* 75: pp. 25–36.
12 Loomis, op cit., p. 209, adapted from Shettel, Harris H. and P. C. Reilly (1968) "An Evaluation of Existing Criteria for Judging the Quality of Science Exhibits," *Curator* 11, 2: pp. 137–53.

7 Storyline and text development

1 Matelic, Candace T. (1984) "Successful Interpretive Planning," video, Nashville, TN: American Association for State and Local History.
2 Kerans, John (1989) "Writing with Style," *ITC Desktop* 2 (May–June): pp. 79–80.
3 Serrell, Beverly (1985), *Making Exhibit Labels: A Step-by-Step Guide*, Nashville, TN: American Association for State and Local History, p. 65.

Glossary

1 Ferree, H. (ed.) (n.d.) *Groot praktijkboek voor effectieve communicatie*, Antwerp, pp. 13–15.
2 Verhaar, Jan and Han Meeter (1989) *Project Model Exhibitions*, Holland: Reinwardt Academie, p. 26.
3 International Council of Museums (ICOM) (1990) *Statutes*, page 1, Article 1 – Name and Legal Status, paragraph 1.
4 Maslow, Abraham H. (1954) *Motivation and Personality* New York: Harper & Row.
5 ICOM, op. cit., page 1, Article 2 – Definitions, paragraph 1.
6 Mitchell, Arnold (1983) *The Nine American Lifestyles*, New York: Warner Books.

Bibliography

Adams, G. D. (1953) *Museum Public Relations*, vol. 2, AASLH Management Series, Nashville, TN: American Association for State and Local History. ISBN 0-910050-65-1.

Alexander, Edward P. (1973) *Museums in Motion*, Nashville, TN: American Association for State and Local History. ISBN 0-910050-35-X.

Alt, M. B. and K. M. Shaw (1984) "Characteristics of Ideal Museum Exhibits," *British Journal of Psychology* 75: pp. 25–36.

American Association of Museums (1992) *The Audience in Exhibition Development*, AAM Course Proceedings, Washington, DC: American Association of Museums.

— (1984) *Museums for a New Century*, Washington, DC: American Association of Museums. ISBN 0-931201-08-X.

Atlas, James (1965) "Beyond Demographics," *The Atlantic Monthly* (October).

Barker, R. G. (1963) *The Stream of Behavior*, New York: Appleton-Century-Crofts.

— (1965) "Explorations in Ecological Psychology," *American Psychologist* 20: pp. 1–14.

Belcher, Michael (1991) *Exhibitions in Museums*, Leicester: Leicester University Press. ISBN 0-87474-913-1.

Berkowitz, Julie S. (1986) "Extending the Collaborative Spirit at the Philadelphia Museum of Art," *Museum News* 65, 1 (October/November): pp. 28–35.

Berry, John D. (1992) "A Brief Glossary of Type," *Aldus Magazine* 3, 3 (March/April): pp. 49–52.

Bitgood, Steve (ed.) (1988) *Visitor Studies – 1988,* Jacksonville, AL: Center for Social Design.

Bloch, Milton J. (1968) "Labels, Legends, and Legibility," *Museum News* 47, 3 (November): pp. 13–17.

Burstein, David and Frank Stasiowski (1982) *Project Management for the Design Professional*, London: Whitney Library of Design/Watson-Gupthill Publications. ISBN 0-8230-7434-X.

Chadbourne, Christopher (1991) "A Tool for Storytelling," *Museum News* 70, 2 (March/April): pp. 39–42.

Cole, Peggy (1984) "Piaget in the Galleries," *Museum News* 63, 1 (October): pp. 1–4.

Conroy, Pete (1988) "Chapter 20: Cheap Thrills and Quality Learning," in Steve Bitgood (ed.) *Visitor Studies – 1988*, Jacksonville, AL: Center for Social Design, pp. 189–91.

Ferree, H. (ed.) (n.d.) *Groot praktijkboek voor effectieve communicatie*, Antwerp.

Finn, David (1985) *How to Visit a Museum*, New York: Harry N. Abrams. ISBN 0-8109-2297-5.

Flacks, Niki and Robert W. Rasberry (1982) "So to Speak," *American Way Magazine* (September): pp. 106–8.

Gentle, Keith (1978) "From Where Do We Begin?" *Art Education* 31, 2 (February): pp. 4–5.

Glicksman, Hal (1972) "A Guide to Art Installations," *Museum News* 50, 2 (February): pp. 22–7.

Halio, Marcia Peoples (1991) "Writing Verbally," *Aldus Magazine* 2, 6 (September): p. 64.

Heine, Aalbert (1981) "Making Glad the Heart of Childhood," *Museum News* 60, 2 (November/December): pp. 23–6.

— (1984a) "It Is Not Enough," Corpus Christi Museum (October).

— (1984b) "Teaching the Easy Way," Corpus Christi Museum (October).

Hood, Marilyn G. (1983) "Staying Away: Why People Choose Not to Visit Museums," *Museum News* 61, 4 (April): pp. 50–7.

— (1984) "Museum Marketing to New Audiences," *Proceedings from a Mountain-Plains Regional Museum Association Workshop* (October).

— (1986) "Getting Started in Audience Research," *Museum News* 64, 3: pp. 24–31.

International Council of Museums (ICOM) (1986) *Public View: The ICOM Handbook of Museum Public Relations*, Paris: International Council of Museums. ISBN 92-9012-107-6.

— (1990) *Statutes*, Paris: International Council of Museums.

Karp, Ivan and Steven D. Lavine (1990) *Exhibiting Cultures*, Washington, DC: Smithsonian Institution. ISBN 1-56098-021-4.

Kavanagh, G. (ed.) (1991) *Museum Languages*, Leicester: Leicester University Press. ISBN 0-1-7185-1359-2.

Kelly, James (1991) "Gallery of Discovery," *Museum News* 70, 2 (March/April): pp. 49–52.

Kerans, John (1989) "Writing with Style," *ITC Desktop* 2, (May–June): pp. 79–80.

Klein, Larry (1986) *Exhibits: Planning and Design*, New York: Madison Square Press. ISBN 0-942604-18-0.

Konikow, Robert B. (1987) *Exhibit Design*, New York: PBC International. ISBN 0-86636-001-8.

Kulik, Gary (1989) "Clarion Call for Criticism," *Museum News* 68, 6 (November/December): pp. 52–6.

Lawless, Benjamin (1958) "Museum Installations of a Semi-Permanent Nature," *Curator* 1: pp. 81–90.

Lewis, Ralph H. (1968) "Effective Exhibits – A Search for New Guidelines," *Museum News* 46, 1 (January): pp. 37–45.

Loomis, Ross J. (1983) "Four Evaluation Suggestions to Improve the Effectiveness of Museum Labels," *Texas Historical Commission* (July): p. 8.

— (1987) *Museum Visitor Evaluation: New Tool for Management*, Nashville, TN: American Association for State and Local History. ISBN 0-910050-83-X.

Malaro, Marie C. (1979) "Collections Management Policies," *Museum News* 58, 1 (November/December): p. 4.

Maslow, Abraham H. (1954) *Motivation and Personality*, New York: Harper & Row.

Matelic, Candace T. (1984) "Successful Interpretive Planning," video, Nashville, TN: American Association for State and Local History.

Maxwell, Sue (1980) "Museums are Learning Laboratories for Gifted Students," *Teaching Exceptional Children* 12, 4 (Summer): pp. 154–9.

Miles, R. S. (ed.) (1982) *The Design of Educational Exhibits*, London: Allen & Unwin. ISBN 0-04-069002-4 AACR2.

Mitchell, Arnold (1983) *The Nine American Lifestyles*, New York: Warner Books.

Morris, Rudolph E. (1962) "Leisure Time and the Museum," *Museum News* 41, 4 (December): pp. 17–21.

Motylewski, Karen (1990) "A Matter of Control," *Museum News* 69, 2 (March/April): pp. 64–7.

NAME (1990) "Materials and Procedures for Producing Exhibit Graphics," *AAM Annual Meeting Proceedings* (May).

Nash, George (1975) "Art Museums as Perceived by the Public," *Curator* 18, 1: pp. 55–67.

Neal, Armenta (1976) *Exhibits for the Small Museum*, Nashville, TN: American Association for State and Local History. ISBN 0-910050-23-6.

— (1987) *Help for the Small Museum*, 2nd edn, Boulder, CO: Pruett Publishing Company. ISBN 0-87108-720-0.

Norris, Patrick (1985) *History by Design*, Austin, TX: Texas Association of Museums.

Olkowski, William, Sheila Daar and Helga Olkowski (1991) *Common-Sense Pest Control*, Newton, CT: The Taunton Press. ISBN 0-942391-63-2.

Oppenheimer, Frank (1982) "Exploring in Museums," *The Colonial Williamsburg Interpreter* 3 (November): pp. 1–4.

Padfield, Tim and Hopwood Erhardt (1982) *Trouble in the Store*, London: International Institute for Conservation of Historic and Artistic Works.

Rabinowitz, Richard (1991) "Exhibit as Canvas," *Museum News* 70, 2 (March/April): pp. 34–8.

Ramsey, Charles G. and Harold R. Sleeper (1970) *Architectural Graphic Standards*, 6th edn, New York: John Wiley & Sons. ISBN 0-471-70780-5.

Reeve, James K. (1986) *The Art of Showing Art*, Tulsa, OK: HCE Publications/Council Oak Books. ISBN 0-933031-04-1.

Rice, Danielle (1989) "Examining Exhibits,"*Museum News* 68, 6 (November/December): pp. 47–50.

Schouten, Frans (1983a) "Target Groups and Displays in Museums," in Piet Pouw, Frans Schouten and Rozlin Guthrie (eds) *Exhibition Design as an Educational Tool*, Holland: Reinwardt Academie.

— (1983b) "Visitor Perception: The Right Approach," in Piet Pouw, Frans Schouten and Rozlin Guthrie (eds) *Exhibition Design as an Educational Tool*, Holland: Reinwardt Academie.

Schroeder, Fred E. H. (1983) "Food for Thought: A Dialogue about Museums," *Museum News* 61, 4 (April): pp. 34–7.

Screven, C. G. (1976) "Exhibit Evaluation: A Goal-Referenced Approach," *Curator* 19, 4: pp. 271–90.

— (1977) "Some Thoughts on Evaluation," in Linda Draper (ed.), *The Visitor and the Museum*, Washington, DC: American Association of Museums.

— (1985) "Exhibitions and Information Centers: Some Principles and Approaches," *Curator* 29: pp. 109–37.

— (1990) "Uses of Evaluation Before, During, and After Exhibit Design," *ILVS Review* 1, 2: pp. 37–66.

Serrell, Beverly (1985) *Making Exhibit Labels: A Step-by-Step Guide*, Nashville, TN: American Association for State and Local History. ISBN 0-910050-64-3.

Shettel, Harris H. (1973) "Exhibits: Art Form or Educational Medium?" *Museum News* 52: pp. 32–41.

— (1989) "Front-End Evaluation: Another Useful Tool," *Annual Conference Proceedings*, Pittsburgh, PA: AAZPA: pp. 434–9.

Shettel, Harris H. and P. C. Reilly (1968) "An Evaluation of Existing Criteria for Judging the Quality of Science Exhibits," *Curator* 11, 2: pp. 137–53.

Smithsonian Institution (1987) *Disabled Museum Visitors: Part of Your General Public*, video, Washington, DC: Office of Museum Programs, Smithsonian Institution.

Stark, Robert A. (1983) "Interpretive Exhibit Design," video, American Association for State and Local History.

Stolow, Nathan (1977) *The Microclimate: A Localized Solution*, Washington, DC: American Association of Museums.

— (1986) *Conservation and Exhibitions*, London: Butterworth & Co. ISBN 0-408-01434-2

— (1987) *Conservation and Exhibitions: Packing, Transport, Storage, and Environmental Considerations*, London: Butterworth & Co. ISBN 0-408-01434-2.

Thompson, G. (1978) *The Museum Environment*, London: Butterworth & Co. ISBN 0-408-70792-5.

Tinkel, Kathleen (1992) "Typographic 'Rules'," *Aldus Magazine* 3, 3 (March/April): pp. 32–5.

Verhaar, Jan and Han Meeter (1989) *Project Model Exhibitions*, Holland: Reinwardt Academie.

Volkert, James W. (1991) "Monologue to Dialogue," *Museum News* 70, 2 (March/April): pp. 46–8.

Vukelich, Ronald (1984) "Time Language for Interpreting History Collections to Children," *Museum Studies Journal* 1, 4 (Fall): pp. 44–50.

Witteborg, Lothar P. (1991) *Good Show!*, 2nd edn, Baltimore: Smithsonian Traveling Exhibitions Service. ISBN 0-86528-007-X.

Wolf, Robert L. (1980) "A Naturalistic View of Evaluation," *Museum News* 58, 1 (September): pp. 39–45.

Wolf, Robert L. and Barbara L. Tymitz (1979) *A Preliminary Guide for Conducting Naturalistic Evaluation in Studying Museum Environments*, Washington, DC: Office of Museum Programs, Smithsonian Institution.

Zycherman, Lynda A. (ed.) (1988) *A Guide to Museum Pest Control*, Washington, DC: Association of Systematics Collections. ISBN 0-942924-14-2.

Index